JOURNEY
WITH A
GIANT

JOURNEY WITH A GIANT

CHOOSE YOUR GUIDE, PURSUE YOUR PURPOSE, AND GROW IN YOUR WALK WITH GOD

LORI G. MELTON

WATERBROOK

WaterBrook

An imprint of the Penguin Random House Christian Publishing Group,
a division of Penguin Random House LLC
1745 Broadway, New York, NY 10019

waterbrookmultnomah.com
penguinrandomhouse.com

A WaterBrook Trade Paperback Original

Trade Paperback ISBN 978-0-593-60206-5
Ebook ISBN 978-0-593-60207-2

LIBRARY OF CONGRESS CATALOGING-IN-PUBLICATION DATA
Names: Melton, Lori G. author
Title: Journey with a giant: choose your guide, pursue your purpose, and grow in your walk with God / Lori G. Melton.
Description: New York, NY: WaterBrook, [2025] | Includes bibliographical references.
Identifiers: LCCN 2025008138 | ISBN 9780593602065 trade paperback | ISBN 9780593602072 ebook
Subjects: LCSH: Rogers, Fred | Christian life | Spiritual formation
Classification: LCC BV4501.3 .M456 2025
LC record available at https://lccn.loc.gov/2025008138

Printed in the United States of America on acid-free paper

1st Printing

The authorized representative in the EU for product safety and compliance is Penguin Random House Ireland, Morrison Chambers, 32 Nassau Street, Dublin D02 YH68, Ireland. https://eu-contact.penguin.ie

BOOK TEAM: Production editor: Helen Macdonald • Managing editor: Julia Wallace • Production manager: Mark Maguire • Copy editor: Carrie Krause • Proofreaders: Kayla Fenstermaker, Drew Goter

Book design by Simon M. Sullivan

For details on special quantity discounts for bulk purchases,
contact specialmarketscms@penguinrandomhouse.com.

To Bryan, the love of my life.
Thank you for inviting me to walk with you so many years ago.
Here's to many more miles ahead.
Yours always,
L

CONTENTS

SEASON THREE—PLAY

SEASON FOUR—TRANSFORM

INTRODUCTION TO THE JOURNEY

Since we are surrounded by such a great cloud of witnesses, let us throw off everything that hinders and the sin that so easily entangles. And let us run with perseverance the race marked out for us, fixing our eyes on Jesus, the pioneer and perfecter of faith. For the joy set before him he endured the cross, scorning its shame, and sat down at the right hand of the throne of God.

—Hebrews 12:1–2

What does it mean to walk with a spiritual giant? To spend a few months or even a few years intentionally learning from a single spiritual mother or father? Is this practice biblical? How can it deepen our faith? Can it really bring us closer to God? Will it help us discover and pursue our purpose?

As believers, we long to become all God created us to be. We know God has called us to a unique purpose meant to give Him glory and point others to Him during our years on earth. Yet a gap often exists between the purpose God designed for us and our knowledge of how to fulfill it. How, then, do we get from where we are now to where God intends for us to be? What practical steps can we take to pursue our purpose and deepen our relationship with God?

In the book of Hebrews, we read about a "cloud of witnesses"—spiritual giants who have gone before us and stand in heaven cheering us on as we run our own races today. This cloud includes men and women from Jesus's time to the present—martyrs, prophets, missionaries, educators, social workers, homemakers, nurses, and other heroes of the faith who have completed their life's pilgrimage. Having faithfully walked their sacred path from birth to eternity, they have much to offer those of us still on earth. Their writings, art, teachings, and life stories are gifts waiting to be received along life's trail—gifts that will help us figure out who it is God has created each of us to be, what it means to be human, and how we can fulfill our individual purposes. As imperfect humans themselves, these pilgrims aren't meant to be venerated, but they should be embraced as examples of people who can help us fix our eyes more fully on Jesus and bring glory to God.

The practice of walking with a spiritual giant isn't a new concept. For centuries, believers have studied the Scriptures, pored over biographies of strong Christians, and read texts such as *Foxe's Book of Martyrs* to learn and grow in their own faith. Generation after generation of our Catholic brothers and sisters have studied the lives of the saints as part of their faith tradition. And over the years, seminal works by faith leaders such as Saint Augustine, Julian of Norwich, Martin Luther, Susanna Wesley, Dietrich Bonhoeffer, Elisabeth Elliot, and Dallas Willard have become pivotal reference guides for countless believers across Christian denominations.

In the same way that amateur athletes can improve their game by studying the tactics of seasoned players, we can gain fresh perspectives and be strengthened for our race by journeying with the heroes of faith. The example set by these men and women can give us the courage to act when we're terrified, help us stand when we feel weak, encourage us to speak when our mouths feel like sawdust, and teach us how to focus when we're distracted. As we run the race set for us, our eyes on Jesus— the Author and Perfecter of our faith—our spiritual giants can help us take our next step . . . and our next and our next, until we cross that finish line.

WHY THIS JOURNEY?

I know what you might be thinking: *Why should I do something like this when I already attend church, participate in Bible study, and even read the occasional Christian biography?*

I had some of the same questions when the professor of my spiritual formation class introduced me to this ancient practice. To be honest, when she told us to pick a person of faith from history to "walk with" during the course, I was worried that I would get sucked into something that resembled what I thought might be saint worship. Shouldn't I be focused only on Jesus?

Thankfully, my instructors were patient with me and my concerns. I quickly learned that walking with a giant was similar to having a mentor or spiritual director—someone older and wiser whom I could learn from while we both followed Christ. As Paul urged the Corinthians, "Imitate me, as I also imitate Christ" (1 Corinthians 11:1, CSB). I also learned that walking with a giant was not about focusing my eyes on them in worship but being strengthened by their example in my own faithfulness to Christ. Over time, it became clear that choosing a giant was often less about our own decisions and more about the miraculous leading of the Spirit—who knows more about what we need than we do.

As I embarked on my journey with a giant, I began to see benefits in my life. Was I smiling as we shared the trail? Was that a quote from my giant strengthening me in my struggle? Was I really thinking about how my giant lived as I wrestled with my decisions and calling? And it didn't happen only for me. I watched as God divinely worked in similar ways in the lives of my classmates as they journeyed with their giants (including Saint Benedict, Madeleine L'Engle, and John Wesley).

In addition, the importance of choosing only one giant for an extended period of time became abundantly clear. At a time when I was facing a new calling and desperately in need of courage, God led me to Evelyn Underhill. A woman of similar age and calling, who lived in the mid-twentieth century, Evelyn's example of intimacy with God, tenacity, and obedience strengthened me to take similar steps of faithfulness in my calling.

In the following years of my spiritual direction training, I was instructed to choose another giant for two years. Longing to walk alongside someone who was holy but also human, I wrestled with whom I should choose. Finally, I landed on Francis of Assisi, who appealed to me because of his love for simplicity, nature, and people.

While I may have learned bits about my giants' lives and perhaps gleaned a lesson or two from reading a biography and a few of their works, it was the years spent by their side that led to profound transformation. Because of my time with Evelyn and Francis—which introduced me to the full gamut of their spiritual practices, habits, strengths, and weaknesses—I gained new perspectives that brought healing to my relationships, a deeper intimacy with God, and more empathy for myself and others.

Over time, the Holy Spirit used the journey with my giants to work the changes in me that I had always longed for: to discover and take new steps in my purpose, to overcome hurdles—where I'd been stuck in my faith and relationships—and to become more of the person I was created to be. Years after the conclusion of my first giant journeys, I'm still amazed at how, almost daily, God continues to shape my life through the lessons I learned while walking with Evelyn Underhill and Francis of Assisi.

Several months after completing my journey with Francis, I realized I missed having a giant in my life and decided to choose another one. This time, God led me to Mister Fred Rogers, and the resulting journey has had a tremendous impact on my life. I kept a careful record of my year with Mister Rogers, and those notes sparked the creation of the book you now hold in your hands. My prayer is that, through these pages, you will learn as much as I did from this extraordinary man and that my experience will guide you on a journey of your own.

HOW TO USE THIS BOOK

This book provides a template for the yearlong "giant journey." You can walk alongside me month by month with Mister Rogers, or you can choose a different giant and follow the principles and steps I lay out. Whatever you decide, your experience is certain to be filled with wonder, adventure, discovery, and growth.

Consider inviting a friend, someone with a spirit of adventure to join you on this journey. Though not required, a friend can multiply the joy and help you stay on the path so you don't miss the spectacular vistas ahead.

To keep the steps in the journey more manageable, the book is divided into four seasons, with each chapter representing a month of the journey. Each month has a unique theme and is further broken down into four weekly articles with journaling prompts. You can begin your journey at any time. As you follow the year format, your relationship with your giant will grow with the changing seasons.

SEASON ONE: DISCOVER

The first season is all about discovery, curiosity, and excitement, beginning from the moment you choose your giant. As you set out on your journey, get to know your giant through an easy-read book, film, YouTube video, or podcast series. Take it slow, being intentional not to rush through this early stage. Consider picking up a biography or other deeper-dive resources as the season progresses.

SEASON TWO: PERSEVERE

After getting to know your giant in season 1, you'll dig even deeper, moving beyond casual acquaintance to true friendship and appreciation for what this person is bringing to your life. You may not have spent this much time studying one person before, so you may be wondering if it's time to move on. But hold steady. This is where the journey gets good, as you move from gathering information to experiencing growth!

SEASON THREE: PLAY

After six months of careful study, use this season to step into the sunshine for a season of play! In this "comfortable" stage of your relationship, take the pressure off big intentions and allow yourself to follow rabbit trails. Explore your giant's journals, artwork, hobbies, or music—or even the writings of their friends and mentors—and discover the influences that transformed *them* even as the divine work continues in you during this relaxed season.

SEASON FOUR: TRANSFORM

By the last stage of the journey, you'll have covered all the broad categories and many of the nuances of your giant's life, unearthed fascinating facts, and collected compelling quotes. The changes that your spirit has been longing for from the beginning of the journey will begin to rise to the surface, inspired by persistent themes and characteristics of your giant as well as by the Spirit's shaping. You might see your prayers for healing or deliverance answered or notice yourself looking at people, the world, and your life differently. After months of faithfulness to the journey, you will begin to notice transformation.

WHAT TO EXPECT

To ensure this journey is easily accessible, each month follows a predictable format, with the aim being consistent engagement and step-by-step growth alongside your giant. In light of these goals, each month begins with these helpful sections:

- **Steps Along the Trail:** an overview of instructions and tasks for the month
- **Journey with Fred:** a list of suggested Mister Rogers resources to explore in that month*
- **Trail Guide:** a template for recording your focus and goals for the month ahead, keeping track of the resources you plan to explore, and jotting down your reflections and experiences throughout the month's journey

Once you have a clear picture of what to expect for the month as a whole, you can dive into the weekly sections, which include . . .

---

* As a reminder, if you have chosen to journey with a different giant, you can skip this section or use it to spark ideas for the resources you could use with your own giant.

- an opening quote
- the topical essay for the week, often incorporating a story from Mister Rogers's life
- one or more journal prompts for reflection

Within each month, you'll also encounter brief testimonials from other pilgrims who have experienced the giant journey. These segments usually correspond to the primary focus in the week or month where they appear, and they are meant to inspire and encourage you in your own journey.

Since the giant journey is similar to a physical pilgrimage, each month closes with a Pilgrimage Principle—a creative imagining of the Camino de Santiago in Spain, which allows you to see the progress on your spiritual journey as it relates to a physical pilgrimage. The principle is followed by a Mile Marker—a space to pause and reflect on the figurative distance you have traveled before you step into the next month. This section includes . . .

- **Final Steps on the Trail:** suggested tasks for concluding the month
- **Reflection:** journal prompts to record the highlights of the month
- **Pilgrim Prayer:** a blessing to end that month's journey and to carry with you into the next
- **Travelogue:** a free-flow writing space to journal any thoughts or revelations

YOUR JOURNEY

Perhaps you picked up this book because you're feeling stuck in your spiritual life, boxed into your small cul-de-sac of faith, or wounded by circumstances that have caused you to wander away from God. Maybe your heart longs for a revitalized relationship with Him. Or you might feel strong in your faith, but you're eager to go even deeper. Whatever your story looks like, this practice is for you.

When your journey is complete, you will have traveled a year with your giant. You will have learned about your giant's life, been introduced to their mentors, and witnessed how they overcame challenges and strengthened their faith. Along the way, you will likely have deepened your relationship with God, unearthed insights about yourself, and taken new steps in your purpose.

Every journey is unique. However yours unfolds, may the Lord guide and bless you during this year with your giant. May He awaken you to the active part He desires to play in your life, illuminate the purpose He has for you, and draw you ever closer to Himself as you move forward on the path of becoming all He has created you to be

Enjoy the journey!

SEASON ONE

DISCOVER

DREAM, PLAN, PREPARE

My introduction to the idea of spiritual giants was profound. It was as if I were a child standing out in the cold, looking in the windows at a world full of color, sound, warmth, and wonder. As amazing as my walk with God had been for my first fifty years, this was an invitation into something I had only felt a longing for, without knowing what it was I had been missing. Here were people who lived in a way I wanted to learn how to do. Voices calling me deeper.

—Chris Slabbekoorn, spiritual director (Giant: Hadewijch of Antwerp, poet, mystic, 1200–1260)

STEPS ALONG THE TRAIL

As you take the first steps of the journey, remember to start slow, using the focus points below as a guide:

☐ Choose your giant.

☐ Become familiar with the trail guide.

☐ Decide how you will begin your journey and set your focus for the month.

☐ Complete the weekly journal prompts and the trail guide.

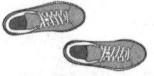 ## JOURNEY WITH FRED

Check out these resources if you've chosen Mister Rogers as your giant:
- *I'm Proud of You: My Friendship with Fred Rogers* by Tim Madigan
- *A Beautiful Day in the Neighborhood,* 2019 film

TRAIL GUIDE

Focus: What is your primary focus for this month? How is God directing your journey?

Media: What are you reading, watching, or listening to as you engage with your giant this month?

Quotes: What meaningful quotes would you like to remember from this month?

Experiences: What new places, activities, or events are you experiencing this month because of your giant?

Faith: In what ways has your giant drawn you closer to God this month? What spiritual practices have you engaged in as a result of your giant journey?

Sticky Points: What questions or topics might you want to explore more later?

CHOOSING A GIANT

As iron sharpens iron,
so one person sharpens another.

—Proverbs 27:17

A giant can come from any area of your life. He or she just needs to be someone who inspires you, exhibits characteristics you greatly admire, and possesses sincere Christian faith. You can trust the Spirit to guide you to the person you most need to learn from in your current season, whatever it may be. Even if you don't feel complete clarity about the giant you're drawn to choose, remember that many times God is working in ways we don't fully understand. He can use anyone and anything to transform our hearts and renew our minds.

After years of walking with different giants, I started keeping a list of powerful heroes of the faith who I thought I might want to journey with one day. I had grown accustomed to sharing life with spiritual companions, taking them my questions and fears, and letting their lives speak into mine. Before learning this practice, I navigated my Christian walk with an individualistic mindset; now I felt lonely without a giant by my side.

I was led to Mister Rogers after viewing a film about his life. Inspired by the powerful way he lived, his love for people, his slow way of talking, his gift of listening, his deep faith, I was eager to know more. I knew the Spirit was nudging me to learn from this amazing man.

For you, the giant you're called to might be someone from history who fascinates you, someone you read about in a book, or someone you heard mentioned on a podcast. The person you choose should also be someone who has completed their race. In other words, just like the spiritual giants in Hebrews 11, your giant for this journey must be someone who has already passed on to heaven.

After you've completed your first giant journey, you can always come back to the beginning and choose a new giant. One of the joys of this practice is that it will be vastly different with each new faith hero you pick. So don't worry too much about choosing the "right" person for your first journey.

Here are a few basic guidelines to help you narrow down your choice: First, ask God to give you wisdom and lead you to the giant He has chosen specifically for you. Second, think about what characteristics you find yourself eager to grow in, what purpose or calling you've been sensing from God, what wounds have been keeping you in dysfunctional patterns, and what diverse voices you've been longing to learn from to broaden your own perspective.

Once you clarify your longings, calling, and struggles, research the believers of the past who may have wrestled with similar things. Imagine how God might want to shape you through the example of a faithful believer who has gone before you and whose life could inspire you to become who He created you to be. Think of it this way:

- If your heart burns for world peace, what if you spent a year with Martin Luther King, Jr.?
- If you're a woman in authority, what would you give for a year at Queen Elizabeth II's side?
- If you're a mother longing to pour God's love into your children, what would it mean to have a year with Susanna Wesley or Ruth Bell Graham?
- If you're an artist struggling to do your work well, what would the transformation within you look like after spending twelve months immersed in the wisdom and creativity of Madeleine L'Engle, Bach, or Michelangelo?
- If you're called to courageous leadership, what could you learn from a year with George Washington, Desmond Tutu, or Harriet Tubman?

To spark ideas, review the list below and circle anyone who appeals to you. These are just a few of the many worthy spiritual giant candidates you might choose, so don't feel as though you have to pick someone on the list. As I mentioned in the introduction, you're also welcome to journey alongside me, with Mister Rogers as your giant. The principles will be the same.

POSSIBLE SPIRITUAL GIANTS

A. W. Tozer

Abraham Lincoln

Augustine of Hippo

Black Elk

Brother Lawrence

C. S. Lewis

Catherine Booth

Charles Spurgeon

Clara Swain

Corrie ten Boom

D. L. Moody

Dallas Willard

Desmond Tutu

Dietrich Bonhoeffer

Dorothy Day

Edith Schaeffer

Elisabeth Elliot

Eric Liddell

Eugene Peterson

Evelyn Underhill

Fannie Lou Hamer

Fanny Crosby

Francis of Assisi

Frederick Douglass

Friedrich von Hügel

George Washington

George Washington Carver

Hannah More

Harriet Tubman

Henri Nouwen

Hildegard of Bingen

Howard Thurman

Hudson Taylor

John Calvin

Jonathan Edwards

Josephine Butler

Julian of Norwich

Katharina von Bora

Madeleine L'Engle

Martin Luther

Mother Teresa

Norman Vincent Peale

Oswald Chambers

Queen Elizabeth II

Rich Mullins

Sojourner Truth

Susanna Wesley

As you continue to reflect on your choice of giant, consider these additional questions:

- Is there anyone else from history who fascinates you and who you're eager to learn more about?
- Are there any real-life people that you've read about in books or seen in movies who profoundly inspire or intrigue you?
- Have any Christians you greatly admire "shown up" in your life one way or another more than once lately?

Is one name flashing in neon lights? If not, that's okay. Give it a little more time and prayer, and observe over the next few days who rises to the top. Wanting to choose the right person can feel unsettling, but try not to worry. Hold the process lightly and allow God to guide you to the giant He has chosen for you.

When you finalize your choice, write your giant's name on the line below.

My spiritual giant for this journey will be

_____.

JOURNAL

- Why did you choose this giant? What drew you to him or her? What characteristics, passions, accomplishments, or struggles led you to this choice?

- What three things are you most interested in gleaning as you walk with this person?

- What is your prayer for your journey?

WEEK TWO

LET'S DO THIS!

When I think of Robert Frost's poems, . . . I feel the support of someone who is on my side, . . . someone who says, "I've been there, and it's okay to go on."

—FRED ROGERS, *The World According to Mister Rogers*

Wanting something lighthearted at the start of my giant journey, I ordered *I'm Proud of You,* which tells the story of the friendship between Mister Rogers and reporter Tim Madigan, the book's author. Each night, I read a few pages and just let myself enjoy the experience. Knowing my giant and I had a year together, I felt in no hurry. My focus was simply to read an easygoing story to begin getting acquainted with Fred.

As you begin your own journey, familiarize yourself with the trail guide at the beginning of each month. Using it as a template, prayerfully determine your focus for the month and then add any books, films, or podcasts under "Media." Don't worry about recording any meaningful quotes, experiences, spiritual practices, or sticky points yet. You can fill those in later.

In the first month, begin with the resource that most intrigues you. (Remember, if you chose Mister Rogers as your giant, you can use the resources I suggest at the beginning of each month in the section labeled "Journey with Fred.") As the months proceed, you may be led to delve into other options. Don't worry about checking off any set number of study resources or experiences. One pilgrim chose Brother Lawrence as his spiritual giant because he had written only one short book. Instead of devouring as many resources as possible, this person was profoundly changed by savoring just one.

To help you get started, here are some options:

- Read a lighthearted book about your giant, a biography, or a book written by your giant.
- Listen to a podcast series about your giant.
- Dig into a YouTube channel that covers the life of your giant or a topic they were interested in.

Try to begin in a relaxed way. If reading a text, avoid underlining or dog-earing pages at this stage. Read *lectio divina* style the first time through, simply enjoying the experience without trying to "get anything out of it." If you read the book again, be a little more intentional and maybe keep a pen or highlighter handy. Pause with each thought that intrigues you and jot in the margins, write down meaningful quotes, and journal your reflections in the travelogue pages provided in this book. If you come across something that puzzles you or requires more research, include that in the "Sticky Points" section of your monthly trail guide. Keep circling back to the trail guide throughout the month.

As you move forward, spend fifteen to thirty minutes a few times a week with your giant. The most common way to do this is by reading your chosen resource or listening to an audiobook or podcast. Try to find consistent times that work for you, whether that is in the morning, before bed, when you're driving, or while you do chores around the house. As you engage with your giant, pay attention to the things that stir you. Some days may be delightful, bringing serendipitous moments of connection, while others might be challenging, revealing, convicting, or even painful. Trust that the Lord is leading you in this process and He has you on the right path.

JOURNAL

- How are you feeling led to begin?

- What resource(s) will you be exploring?

DESPERATE FOR A GUIDE

I was in a difficult season of my life—in my late thirties, ten or twelve years into pastoral ministry—and floundering. Though desperate for an older, wiser guide, I'd had trouble finding a spiritual director and felt cast out into the wide sea on a dinghy. Then a little book of Fénelon's letters arrived from a friend.

What could François Fénelon, a French archbishop, born in 1651, who served as an adviser and tutor to Louis XIV's grandson, have to say to this American pastor living in the early 2000s?

As it turned out, Fénelon had a lot to say about the terrain my soul was in as I asked the questions, "What do I do with this darkness I feel? Or this sadness? I want to know God, but I feel like I'm floundering. I'm trying really hard. Where is God?"

I think it was C. S. Lewis who said there were old voices in books who became guides for him. I'm not sure I understood that until I encountered Fénelon. For a season, he was very much that for me.

The experience was actually quite liberating, because it opened my eyes to see that I also have these other voices that are available to me if I allow them to speak into my life.

—Winn Collier, author, Eugene Peterson Center for
Christian Imagination (Giant: François Fénelon,
archbishop, theologian, poet, 1651–1715)

YOUR TAGLINE

It's not the honors and the prizes and the fancy outsides of life which ultimately nourish our souls. It's the knowing that we can be trusted, that we never have to fear the truth, that the bedrock of our very being is good stuff. . . . What is essential about you that is invisible to the eyes?

—FRED ROGERS, in *New York Times Magazine* article "The Mister Rogers No One Saw" by Jeanne Marie Laskas

Have you ever seen the movie *A Beautiful Day in the Neighborhood*, starring Tom Hanks? It tells the story of reporter Tom Junod and the healing relationship he experienced with Fred Rogers. As I mentioned in week 2, the first book I selected on my journey with Mister Rogers was about a reporter's relationship with him. I assumed the author was the same reporter the movie was based on, because, with all the demands on Fred's time, how could he have had this level of relationship with more than one? But, I was wrong. The reporter in the book was Tim Madigan and the one in the movie was Tom Junod.

Like Tom, Tim met Mister Rogers because of an article Tim was assigned to write. He flew to Pittsburgh on a Friday to interview Fred and ended up enjoying his company for three days. Fred spent all of Saturday with Tim and then invited him to church the next morning, where Tim sat with Fred and his family. When it was time for Tim to leave, Fred walked him to his car, expressing how happy he was that they had become friends. As he walked away, Fred turned around with a warm call of "Goodbye" and the "friend" hand motion in sign language. Instead of doing the interview and keeping the reporter at arm's length, Fred had opened his heart and life.

What resided at the core of Fred Rogers was no secret. If asked to create a tagline for his life, you would likely include words or phrases such as *unconditional love* or *kindness*. If your giant is someone like Mother Teresa, you might come up with a tagline that references her heart for the poor or includes the word *compassion*. If your giant is a great leader like Teddy Roosevelt, known for his saying "Speak softly and carry a big stick," you might create a tagline that centers on the word *strength*.

As you begin to learn what people said about Fred, think about what those you know and love might say about you. What words would others use to describe you? What characteristics pour from your words and actions during your work and play? How do others see you?

Regardless of what others might say about you, what do *you* want your tagline to be? Who you were created to be is wrapped up in your answer. As God shapes you in walking with your giant, may He bring you a few steps closer to becoming that person.

JOURNAL

- How has your giant shaped what you hope your tagline will be?

A FOURTEENTH-GENERATION DESCENDANT

Choosing my giant was a unique journey. In my seventies, I felt a strong pull to go back and live in the same community where I was raised. I'd been pondering the profound effect our ancestors have on shaping the generations to come, and I longed to be a blessing to my living siblings, children, grandchildren, nieces, nephews, and community.

Through a conversation with my brother and a study of the first Thanksgiving, I discovered something incredible: I am a fourteenth-generation descendant of Lizzie Tilly Howland, one of the original 102 pilgrims on the *Mayflower.*

Lizzie was a woman of extraordinary faith. She bore ten children, and today her descendants number in the millions. Her father and husband were both signers of the Mayflower Compact. In her last will and testament, she bequeathed three books: the family Bible and two works by William Tyndale, a Bible translator and martyr.

As I reflected on the long lineage of Christian faith in my family—my own habit of carrying small New Testaments to give away and my involvement in local elections and country government—I couldn't help but wonder if the seeds planted by my great-great-great-grandparents, John and Lizzie, had been quietly guiding my steps all along.

Through this journey, I have been deeply moved and grateful. And so, I wrote these words as a tribute: "Thank you, Lizzie, for your faithfulness to God. With love, from one of your many, many down-the-line grand-daughters, Linda Joy."

—Linda Wierenga, licensed practical nurse (Giant: Elizabeth Tilley Howland, *Mayflower* pilgrim, 1607–87)

EMBRACING NERDY AND WONDERFUL YOU

You formed my innermost being, shaping my delicate inside and my intricate outside . . . I thank you, God, for making me so mysteriously complex! Everything you do is marvelously breathtaking.

—Psalm 139:13–14, TPT

Many of us have a hidden passion we're hesitant to share with others. Maybe you like playing the kazoo or you've got a thing for knitting. Perhaps you're obsessed with learning other languages or you harbor a deep longing to write a novel one day. Whatever your secret, what if it is the very thing God wants to use?

Consider Fred Rogers. How many hours did he play make-believe with his puppets in his attic? How many scenarios did he act out? How many ventriloquist voices did he create? Do you suppose he dared to tell his teenage friends how he spent his free time?

After graduating from college, Fred realized he was passionate about television. Combining his love for children and education, he allowed his puppets to take center stage on *The Children's Corner*, the first children's show at a newly formed television station. The show revolved around the host, a young girl named Josie Carey, connecting to the hearts of children by pouring out her dreams, hopes, and fears to the puppets.

As Josie faced the camera, Fred knelt below the stage, out of sight, animating the puppets. The conversations between Josie and the puppets felt so real that, afterward, she would often repeat what she had told them to Fred backstage, forgetting that he was the puppeteer and had carried on those conversations with her.

Those puppets spoke about the hard and exciting things in life not only to children but also to the adults watching with them. Later, they would become a vital piece of *Mister Rogers' Neighborhood,* one of the most beloved and powerful children's programs of all time.

Clearly, the nerdiness that most would have scoffed at or quashed was the very thing Fred used to reach millions. Isn't that comforting?

Perhaps you're like me and you've never been the cool one in the crowd. When I want to be the polished professional or smooth public speaker, I tend to be the overly simple and friendly girl, which makes me feel like a little kid in a fifty-five-year-old woman's body.

But no matter how incapable or insecure I might feel sometimes, God designed all these quirks in me just as He designed the ones in Fred Rogers. As a result, when I sit in a spiritual direction appointment and listen to a person's pain, my friendly persona allows them to feel comfortable rather than intimidated. I may not be the sophisticated professional I often wish I could be, but I will happily let that go if I can be an approachable friend instead.

The good news is that God purposefully designed that little nerdy side in each of us, and it is perfect!

JOURNAL

- What quirks might you be hiding that could become blessings to those around you?

- How is your giant helping you embrace the passions God has placed inside you?

PILGRIMAGE PRINCIPLE

FIND YOUR PACE

To be a pilgrim is to be willing to live with the mystery of what will happen both interiorly and exteriorly as one walks day after day after day toward the destination of the sacred site. What happens inside cannot be planned or mapped out in the same way that the physical route is mapped. . . . One simply holds onto the hand of the Great Pilgrim and travels with hope that one day the spiritual benefits of the road will reveal themselves and be understood.

—JOYCE RUPP, *Walk in a Relaxed Manner*

I n the last few years, I've been captivated by the topic of pilgrimage. A pilgrimage is an intentional journey to a sacred site. In the same way, our lives are spiritual pilgrimages from birth to death, leading us toward the sacred destination of our eternal home in heaven.

As you finish your first month with your giant, join me on this imaginary journey along one of the most well-known pilgrimage routes in the world today—the Camino de Santiago, a five-hundred-mile walking pilgrimage across northern Spain. I hope to walk it in person one day, but for now, we can travel in our imagination with our fellow pilgrims.

• • •

The journey has finally begun, and you're still bursting with excitement. But after waking up before dawn on those first few days so you could aggressively rack up the miles, you feel some achiness in your bones and soreness in your muscles. Apparently, finding your way with your giant may take some getting used to. You may wonder, *How exactly do I do this?*

Each person experiences a unique pilgrimage when on the Camino (which translates to "way" or "path"). Some come for the physical challenge and the excitement of spending time outdoors. Others come for the spiritual growth—the daily turning of their hearts to God as they pay attention to the divine movements they notice along the way.

Each pilgrim should also set their own pace. One day, you may walk seventeen miles. But the next, you may find yourself drawn to something along the trail, bidding you to linger and walk only ten. As you move forward, try not to follow anyone else's itinerary. Many pilgrims on the Camino have been handicapped by blisters and muscle strain as they push too hard and walk too fast. Caught up in the early euphoria of the journey, some have had their pilgrimage cut short by injuries from overexertion.

Two Camino pilgrims in their sixties were less physically fit than many others on the trail with them, yet they suffered no blisters or muscle strain. Their secret? "Walking in a relaxed manner." Instead of pressing on to reach the end, they stopped regularly to remove their shoes and socks and to let their feet breathe in the fresh air and sunshine.*

• • •

When you walk in a hurry, your head stays down and you rarely savor the things around you. Like the pilgrim who blisters the whole bottom of their foot by pushing too hard, we can be impatient for our transformation.

But growth takes time.

On the journey with your giant, enjoy finding your own pace. Let go of the fear that you might miss something. Don't be anxious for the next book or experience. Instead, save yourself from the blisters and strained muscles, trust the Guide who has led you here, and walk your own Camino with grace.

---

* Joyce Rupp, *Walk in a Relaxed Manner: Life Lessons from the Camino* (Orbis Books, 2005), 90.

JOURNAL

- When you consider your giant journey, what are your first impressions of your pace? Too fast? Too slow? Just right?

MILE MARKER

The giant journey offers natural moments to pause at the side of the trail. Take time to do this at the end of each month.

FINAL STEPS ON THE TRAIL

- Find a quiet time and place during the last week of the month and ask the Lord to open your eyes to anything He would like you to see. Read through this month's journal sections, review the Pilgrimage Principle, and highlight anything that stands out to you.
- Circle back to the trail guide and fill in any quotes, experiences, spiritual practices, or sticky points you haven't noted yet. Ponder what the Lord has been doing in you this month and write down anything He might be stirring in you.

REFLECTION

Take some time to reflect on the following questions as you wrap up the month. Your answers can be great indicators of what the Spirit might be leading you to focus on in the month ahead.

Summary: What direction did the Lord take you this month? Did your month go like you thought it would? Were there any unexpected leadings, twists, or turns?

Growth: In what areas of your life do you see growth or shifts in your thinking?

Excitement: When you think about your journey, what fills you with energy?

Challenges: What is bothering you? Do you have any unanswered questions or frustrations related to your journey?

PILGRIM PRAYER

Oh Lord, my divine guide and shepherd, thank You for directing me to this journey and faithfully leading me to the giant I have chosen. Help me go at my own pace and grow in my ability to hear Your voice. I know there are many things You want to give me. I long to receive them all. Open my ears, my eyes, and my heart to experience You in this new way, walking with my giant, who faithfully walked with You. Amen.

TRAVELOGUE

....

....

....

....

....

....

....

....

....

....

....

....

....

....

....

....

....

....

....

EARLY DAYS

In the Catholic tradition, it's common for a teacher or writer like my-self to have an "intellectual father" or mother, upon whose founda-tion they build a library of work; Dallas Willard is that for me. I never had the privilege of knowing him personally, but I have read and re-read all of his books over and over and *over*. No human mind has more deeply shaped my view of apprenticeship to Jesus and life as a whole.

—JOHN MARK COMER, PracticingtheWay.org

STEPS ALONG THE TRAIL

In this second month, imagine yourself moving deeper into a friendship that has progressed beyond the acquaintance stage. Use the focus points below as a guide:

- ☐ Continue getting acquainted with the journey and your giant.
- ☐ Keep exploring your resource(s) from the previous month and consider adding a biography or another resource that is intriguing to you.
- ☐ Complete the weekly journal prompts and the trail guide.

 ## JOURNEY WITH FRED

Check out these resources if you're joining the giant journey with Mister Rogers:

- *The Simple Faith of Mister Rogers: Spiritual Insights from the World's Most Beloved Neighbor* by Amy Hollingsworth
- *The Good Neighbor: The Life and Work of Fred Rogers* by Maxwell King
- *The Little Prince* by Antoine de Saint-Exupéry

TRAIL GUIDE

Focus: What is your primary focus for this month? How is God directing your journey?

Media: What are you reading, watching, or listening to as you engage with your giant this month?

Quotes: What meaningful quotes would you like to remember from this month?

Experiences: What new places, activities, or events are you experiencing this month because of your giant?

Faith: In what ways has your giant drawn you closer to God this month? What spiritual practices have you engaged in as a result of your giant journey?

Sticky Points: What questions or topics might you want to explore more later?

DIVINE THREADS

....

Every experience God gives us, every person He puts in our lives is the perfect preparation for a future that only He can see.

—CORRIE TEN BOOM, *The Hiding Place*

O ne of Fred Rogers's most notable contributions and lasting legacies was the way he brought silence to a noisy world. As a firm believer in the power of silence, he regularly practiced silent, centering prayer. In his leisure time, he lived a largely quiet life through his pursuits of reading, swimming, and reflection. He included moments of silence in his popular children's program, *Mister Rogers' Neighborhood*. And when he was asked to speak at the White House, he began his presentation by inviting the group to pause for ten seconds of silence. He then asked the audience to think of someone who had made a positive impact on their lives and to offer silent gratitude for that person.

Over the last few years, God has consistently been directing me to embrace *silence* and *slowness*. I seem to encounter these terms everywhere—from books and sermons to Bible study and personal experiences. So I shouldn't have been surprised to find them again, this time in the first chapter of Amy Hollingsworth's book *The Simple Faith of Mister Rogers*, where she cited silence as the foundation of Fred's spiritual life. What a revelation that was to me as I listened to this passage while making dinner one evening. Before I began my journey with Mister Rogers, I had no idea these two characteristics were hallmarks of how he lived. God was adding another layer to the crafting He wanted to do in my soul.

Nothing in our lives happens by chance. Every person we meet and every experience we have are divine threads of the plan God is weaving throughout our lives. When you see consistent themes emerge on your journey, open your eyes and ears and receive what He is sending your way. These reemerging topics are evidence of your faithful Father continuing the good work He began in you that will go on, if you are open to it, until your last day.

JOURNAL

- What divine threads that God has been weaving in your life are coming to the surface again, as you walk with your giant?

- What is your prayer as you notice these things?

AN ANCIENT HERO OF THE FAITH

So often in my experience within the Protestant Christian tradition, I have found a significant gulf between my spiritual journey and that of the people described on the pages of Scripture. But I have found encouragement from the women and men who have also studied the stories and teachings of Jesus over the past two thousand years and have wrestled with and explored what it means to be a Christ follower in different times.

It is perhaps ironic, then, that I was drawn to Origen, a spiritual giant from the earliest years of Christianity. I began to study this ancient writer and theologian because so many of my present-day spiritual giants referred to him. As I read his writings and commentaries for myself, Origen revealed himself to me in ways that transcended history, theology, or intellectual understanding. It felt as though he was making himself known to my consciousness in ways that went beyond what was written on his ancient pages. There was a connection, and I came to recognize and appreciate the great cloud of witnesses and their willingness to be present to me. Not only was Jesus accompanying me on my spiritual journey, but spiritual giants such as Origen were as well.

—Richard Bates, MD, chief medical officer, spiritual director (Giant: Origen of Alexandria, writer and theologian, ca. 185–253)

FOMO

God is always doing 10,000 things in your life, and you may be aware
of three of them.

—JOHN PIPER, Twitter (now X)

I n the second month of your journey, you may experience doubts about
the giant you have chosen. You may notice other magnificent people
from history and wonder if you should have picked one of them. You
may worry that, by choosing the giant you did, you will miss out on opportunities you might have gained from someone else.

The fear of missing out was definitely a part of my journey with Fred.
Only a few weeks into the walk, I began doubting my choice. (To be
honest, it's not uncommon for me to battle FOMO no matter what I'm
doing.) Was it covetousness? My selfish human nature wanting more,
more, more like a young scrapper scrambling to grab the best food on
the table, afraid there won't be enough to go around? Was it restlessness,
driven by eavesdropping on others' conversations as I walked the trail
and wondering if I should try to maneuver myself to a different partner?
Or was it fear?

- fear that I would be overlooked
- fear that I wasn't my heavenly Father's favorite and that He
  wasn't watching out for me
- fear that no one was watching out for me
- fear that if I didn't claw and scramble for opportunities, my life
  wouldn't turn out the way I had planned

- fear that I wouldn't become what I was meant to be but would spend my life invisible—a stagehand—while others lived in the limelight

If you've faced some of these same doubts, know that there is no need to fear. God is ordaining all your steps. You are the apple of His eye and His treasured child. He could never forget about you, and He wants more for you than you could ever imagine for yourself.

So set aside your worries about the giant you've chosen and the journey you're on, regardless of whether you perceive anything significant happening or not. Trust that God has guided your decision and allow yourself to let go of fear and fully engage in the experience.

JOURNAL

- How have you struggled with doubts since choosing your giant? What could be underneath those concerns?

THE POWER OF ONE

Sometimes it takes only one act of kindness and caring to change a person's life.

—Jackie Chan

Fred Rogers was painfully shy and different from other kids. He was overweight and non-athletic, he came from an extremely wealthy family, and he was chauffeured to school each morning—the perfect storm for rejection and bullying. As a result, he was lonely and insecure throughout elementary and middle school.

But everything changed during his freshman year of high school when Jim Stumbaugh, the most popular student in school, got injured playing football. Fred's mother suggested that he take Jim's schoolwork to the hospital, so he did. As the boys got to know each other, Fred shared his feelings of rejection, and Jim shared the pain of his father's death. When Jim returned to school, he told everyone "that Rogers kid" was "OK" and invited him to several activities.

That was all Fred needed: just one person who believed in him. By his senior year, Fred was president of the student council and editor of the yearbook.

His story reminded me of a girl named Katie from my high school. As a terrified transfer student, she was having an agonizing time fitting in. She wasn't the prettiest or the coolest. Even though she had been a 4.0 student at her former school, her grades began to plummet when she transferred, and I was asked to tutor her.

The first time we met in an empty classroom, fear and pain were written all over her face. I could sense her hurt over not being accepted or loved and her fear that I would reject her like all the others had. Before we started her assignment, I wanted to show her that I could be a friend. As it turned out, that was all that mattered. Were there a few things in algebra she didn't understand? Maybe. Truthfully, I think she was in the "brilliant" IQ zone and could have tutored me. What she really needed was a friend.

We met a few more times, and I noticed a growing sense of confidence and joy in her. She had found her wings. All she needed, just like Fred, was one person to pay attention to her and affirm her.

Maybe you know someone like Katie or Fred. Or maybe you sometimes feel like Katie or Fred. It's easy to forget how painful it is to be the new kid on the block. Being connected to others is a core part of what it means to be human. When we feel unknown or outside the circle, we can try too hard, act completely out of character, and scold ourselves afterward. If you are in a situation like that, remember to be kind to yourself. And keep your eyes open for the Freds and Katies who need a friend. The world wouldn't be as bright without them, and you could be the one who changes everything on their path to belonging.

JOURNAL

- What story from your giant's life reminds you of a similar one from your own?

A LIFELINE AT SEA

I became acquainted with G. K. Chesterton, the author of *Orthodoxy,* because I wanted to argue with him. I bet that would please him no end. He always loved a good argument—but never a quarrel.

I was nearing the end of my rope with my young, uninformed faith. As a young adult, I had come to know Jesus and was captivated by the ways He loves and the promises He makes and keeps. Among the chief of those promises was that He had come so that I might have life abundantly (John 10:10). But after my baptism, I received very little nourishment to make that abundant life a reality.

I was tossed about on the seas of a mystery that I wasn't prepared to navigate until G. K. Chesterton threw me a lifeline from the good ship *Orthodoxy.* I haven't let go since. As my happy companion and stalwart guide these last couple of decades, G. K. Chesterton's wonder-filled words and jolly worldview have helped make real the ideas I'd dared to hope were true about following Jesus but seldom saw manifested in everyday life.

—Justine Olawsky, education program coordinator, *Renovaré*

(Giant: G. K. Chesterton, writer, philosopher, 1874–1936)

EUREKA!

One of the most essential ways of saying "I love you" is being a receptive listener.

—FRED ROGERS, *The World According to Mister Rogers*

The first small changes inspired by your giant's influence can occur at any time during the early stages of the journey. You might notice yourself pausing before speaking instead of blurting out a response, feeling a sense of peace amid bad news when you would usually unravel, or laughing with a friend when external pressures would typically prevent you from cracking a smile. When you notice the first change, do a little happy dance (inwardly or outwardly). God is beginning to answer your prayers.

During the second month with Mister Rogers, I had my first awakening that things inside me were beginning to change. One morning, as my husband and I were eating breakfast, I was feeling rushed. I had a lot to do and felt like he was taking too long to explain something. Wanting to give my husband a subtle hint to bring the conversation to an end so I could move on with my day, I started clearing the table and doing the dishes. He got the message—he finished talking and left for work.

As I heard the gravel crunch under his tires, I remembered the story of the locker room attendant who worked at the health club where Fred swam every morning. In an interview with one of Fred's biographers, the attendant recounted how Fred had influenced his life. Instead of looking past him like most others did who came to the club, Fred never missed a chance to greet him warmly and pause to chat. Then there was the story of a limo driver who chauffeured Fred to a fancy dinner where he was a featured guest. Fred insisted the driver come in and enjoy the evening too. Countless fans who stopped Fred on the street recounted how he never brushed anyone aside, always giving his undivided attention to each person. No one was ever a nuisance, distraction, or waste of time. He was never in too big of a hurry to be fully attentive to whoever God placed along his path.

As I recalled these stories, I realized I hadn't shown my dear husband love like Fred would have. He hadn't had my full attention, nor had he driven away feeling like the most important person in my world. I was immediately aware that I shouldn't have rushed him along and decided that, next time, I would listen wholeheartedly.

Clearly, God was working through the example of my giant to shape me into the person I longed to be—the person He had created me to be. I could have learned this same principle from a Sunday sermon or a Bible study, but seeing the work of the Spirit exemplified in another person of faith helped drive home the lesson in my mind and heart. Only two months in, and God was already using my giant journey to bring transformation in my life!

JOURNAL

- What small change have you noticed in yourself since you started walking with your giant?

PILGRIMAGE PRINCIPLE

HOLD ON TO THE GIFT

··

When struggling with important decisions . . . we must consult the very author of life, remembering His words to "Ask, seek, and knock." . . . We trust Him to guide us into His will and purpose for our lives.

—PERRY GABBARD, *Stepping Out on an Adventure of Faith*

A week into your glorious Camino pilgrimage, you've passed through quaint villages, visited cathedrals, and crossed both mountains and prairies. You've been breathing in the fresh air, enjoying conversation and laughter with your fellow pilgrims, and savoring the time you've spent in reflection and prayer.

Then, out of nowhere, your euphoria is broken by assaulting thoughts, confusion, and judgment from others. You begin to hear accusatory inner voices saying, *Isn't this pilgrimage a little extravagant? Sure, you can be close to God out on this trail, but couldn't you feel just as close to Him in your own community? What about all that still needs to be done at home and in your church?*

Before you know it, you're doubting your journey and considering whether you should let go of the whole experience. In that moment, your gift from God is in danger of being stolen—right when you're walking what should be the happiest part of your path.

• • •

A few months into my journey, I began wrestling with inner accusations and fear. Doubts about the biblical basis for this practice were nagging at me, causing me to question if I was in danger of idolatry. Even though I still cherished my daily Bible reading and Sunday services, I wondered if the time I'd been spending "fixing my eyes" on Fred should be spent doing what I'd done for the last thirty-plus years of my Christian life: studying the life of Jesus.

Yet when I examined Hebrews 11–12 again, I found assurance that God had clearly given us the cloud of witnesses to help us run our race. For example, musicians and worship leaders today still draw from the psalms of David for inspiration. Pastors and theologians regularly refer to the letters Paul wrote to the early churches. And Christians throughout time have been strengthened by the teachings left behind my ministers, missionaries, and martyrs from previous centuries. As long as we remember that all these saints were humans like us, who are we to tell God He can't use their lives of faith to teach and encourage us in ours?

Anytime we fully embrace the gifts God has for us, the enemy is never far away. I remember the fear I felt when I visited a Pentecostal church for the first time and felt unfamiliar with the volume and worship style. And the way I shook in my boots when I walked into a Catholic center for my first spiritual formation class. No doubt you've experienced similar fears when you've stepped into any calling from God that was unfamiliar or different from what everyone else was doing. Perhaps it was going to counseling or spiritual direction for the first time, participating in a practice like fasting or silence, or responding to a prompting from the Spirit to venture into foreign missions. These ways of growing in our faith can often feel scary or borderline wrong. But perhaps we should instead view them as gifts God is holding out to us so we can continue growing closer to Him.

If you're scared, I understand. It takes courage to step into something new. But God has a lifetime of ways for us to grow in knowing Him. He has led you to this journey because the cloud of witnesses will draw you closer to Jesus, not further away. So even if the Spirit's leading feels unfamiliar or scary at times, trust God and step forward in faith. You never want to miss a gift He is holding out to you.

JOURNAL

- What faith traditions, personal experiences, or other unfamiliar leadings of the Spirit have caused you to fear or doubt this journey?

MILE MARKER

The giant journey offers natural moments to pause at the side of the trail. Take time to do this at the end of each month.

FINAL STEPS ON THE TRAIL

- Find a quiet place (and maybe something to sip!) and review your journal from month 2, highlighting or underlining anything that feels important. Are you surprised at the things that have come up in "conversation" already as you walk with your giant? In these early days of getting to know your giant, what are your first impressions?
- Circle back to your month 2 trail guide and fill in any quotes, experiences, spiritual practices, or sticky points you haven't recorded yet.

REFLECTION

Take some time to reflect on the following questions as you wrap up the month. Your answers can be great indicators of what the Spirit might be leading you to focus on in the month ahead.

Summary: What direction did the Lord take you this month? Did your month go like you thought it would? Were there any unexpected leadings, twists, or turns?

Growth: In what areas of your life do you see growth or shifts in your thinking?

Excitement: When you think about your journey, what fills you with energy?

Challenges: What is bothering you? Do you have any unanswered questions or frustrations related to your journey?

PILGRIM PRAYER

Is it possible, Abba, to truly change? There is a person I want to be, who I believe You've created me to be, and I wonder if it is possible to become that person. Can ingrained habits be broken? I don't know, but if You can create the stars and galaxies, I'm sure my transformation is not too hard for You. Help me, Abba, to believe and step forward in faith. Amen.

TRAVELOGUE

....

....

....

....

....

....

....

....

....

....

....

....

....

....

....

....

....

....

BEYOND SMALL TALK

We are not meant to be as separated as we have become from those who have gone before us and those who will come after. I learned to know and understand my father far more after his death than during his life. Here we are on the border of the tremendous Christian mystery: time is no longer a barrier.

—MADELEINE L'ENGLE, *Walking on Water*

STEPS ALONG THE TRAIL

In the final month of season 1, your giant should start to feel like an old friend. Deepen that relationship this month, using the focus points below as a guide:

- ☐ Write a list of the things you still want to find out or understand better about your giant, which can include the following: upbringing, significant relationships, career, spiritual formation, calling, and faith practices. You can refer to the questions in the first week or come up with your own.
- ☐ Find ways to fill in those gaps in your understanding.
- ☐ Complete the weekly journal prompts and the trail guide..

 ## JOURNEY WITH FRED

Check out this resource if you're joining the giant journey with Mister Rogers:
- *The Good Neighbor: The Life and Work of Fred Rogers* by Maxwell King

TRAIL GUIDE

Focus: What is your primary focus for this month? How is God directing your journey?

Media: What are you reading, watching, or listening to as you engage with your giant this month?

Quotes: What meaningful quotes would you like to remember from this month?

Experiences: What new places, activities, or events are you experiencing this month because of your giant?

Faith: In what ways has your giant drawn you closer to God this month? What spiritual practices have you engaged in as a result of your giant journey?

Sticky Points: What questions or topics might you want to explore more later?

YOUR GIANT'S DNA

··

Most men pursue pleasure with such breathless haste that they hurry past it.

—Søren Kierkegaard, *Either/Or*

As I recognized the importance of these early months in establishing a foundation of understanding who Fred was, I realized there were significant things I still didn't know. So, I decided to return to Maxwell King's biography, *The Good Neighbor*, and reread it more slowly, focusing on the details of Fred's physical, spiritual, and emotional DNA. Other books I had glanced through talked about his adult years and accomplishments. But before jumping into those, I knew I needed to understand what had made Fred who he was at his core and what unique influences had shaped him into America's favorite neighbor.

The giant journey is meant to be slow. It's intentionally called a walk, because when we walk, we have time to notice the details around us. We can see things far away coming steadily closer until they are right next to us and then behind. We have time to process, absorb, and receive.

On a tour, many people jump on a bus and travel from town to town, where guides give them an hour to hustle through the shops and snap pictures, only to board the bus again and speed off to the next stop. These tourists, while covering a lot of ground, will never know all the wonders and details they miss by rushing from one attraction or town to another.

Walking instead of running through our giant journey takes discipline. We may just want to get to the end, where we can experience full transformation, but there's no telling what gems of insight or divine connections we might miss if we rush the process. The giant journey teaches us that the reward is in slowing down on the trail, not racing to the destination. Walking—the pace at which Jesus moved—is the perfect speed to receive all that God has waiting for us.

Instead of hurrying ahead, slow down to make sure that you fully understand the most important pieces that shaped your giant into who they were in spirit, soul, and body. Fill in any gaps in your giant's DNA that you may have missed or skimmed over. And as you prayerfully dig deeper into your chosen resources, consider these questions and any others the Spirit brings to your mind:

1. What was your giant's family like?
2. Who were the most influential adults in their life?
3. Who were they by nature?
4. Who were they by nurture?
5. What were their most formative experiences growing up, either positive or negative?
6. What were their earliest experiences of spiritual formation?
7. What factors planted the seeds of their most significant gifts and calling?

Whether or not you can answer all these questions for your giant already, challenge yourself during the month ahead to maintain a slow pace and to ask God to meet you along the trail.

JOURNAL

- What do you still need to understand about your giant's physical, spiritual, and emotional DNA? (Use the questions above as a guide or jot down your own.)

WHO SHAPED YOUR GIANT?

All of us have special ones who have loved us into being. Would you just take, along with me, ten seconds to think of the people who have helped you become who you are, those who have cared about you and wanted what was best for you in life?

—FRED ROGERS, Lifetime Achievement Award speech, 1997

Fred McFeely Rogers was born to Jim and Nancy Rogers on March 20, 1928, in Latrobe, Pennsylvania. Jim Rogers was a machinist at the McFeely Brick Company when he met Nancy, the owner's beautiful, spunky, intelligent daughter. They married and eventually purchased Latrobe Die Casting, Fullman Manufacturing, and the McFeely Brick Company. Before long, Jim had an office on the sixth floor of one of the tallest buildings in Latrobe and could have easily surrounded himself with all the niceties of life among the elite.

But Jim wasn't like that. As well as being an exceptional businessman, he loved people. Known to regularly visit his factories, he would often greet each of his more than five hundred employees by name and take a genuine interest in their lives.

Nancy, too, poured herself into the people of Latrobe. She gave hundreds of gifts at Christmas and knit a sweater each month for someone on her Christmas list. (Yep, the famous sweaters you see Fred wearing on *Mister Rogers' Neighborhood* were knitted by his mom!) She cooked meals for those in need and volunteered at the hospital. And if there were students who needed shoes or coats, she quietly arranged for the school nurse to send her the bill. She and Jim also loved opening their home to the community for their annual Christmas party.

In addition to being powerfully influenced by his parents, Fred was very close to his maternal grandparents. Nancy "Nana" McFeely always nurtured his musical passion. When Fred was ten, she told him she would buy him a piano. After taking the trolley downtown, Fred picked out his favorite: a 1920 Steinway concert grand costing $3,000—equal to nearly $50,000 today. Fred composed most of the music for *Mister Rogers' Neighborhood* on that piano and moved it to every house he ever lived in.

Fred also adored his grandfather and namesake, Fred Brooks McFeely, whom he affectionately called Ding Dong, after his grandfather taught him the nursery rhyme "Ding Dong Dell." Ding Dong was the one who first encouraged Fred to take risks when he asked permission to climb the stone walls encircling his grandparents' farm, much to the dismay of his mother and grandmother. Later, with scrapes and torn pants, Fred beamed up at his grandfather and told him all about his adventures. As he proudly looked into his grandson's eyes, Ding Dong spoke the words Fred would recite in nearly every episode of *Mister Rogers' Neighborhood:* "You've made this day a special day just by being yourself. Always remember there's just one person in the whole world like you—and I like you the way you are."*

From these stories, it's easy to see how the influence and nurturing of Fred's family and community gloriously converged in shaping him into Mister Rogers. From his father, he learned how to juggle endless responsibilities while still paying attention to each person in front of him. From his mother, he learned how to love a neighborhood and what it looks like to build a community full of helpers. From his grandmother, he learned a love for music and felt empowered to nurture his emotions. From his grandfather, he learned to take risks and to believe that he had something to offer the world that no one else could. And from his

* Fred Rogers, "Guideposts Classics: Fred Rogers on a Grandfather's Love," Guideposts, accessed April 15, 2025, https://guideposts.org/positive-living/health-and-wellness/life-advice/finding-life-purpose/guideposts-classics-fred-rogers-on-a-grandfathers-love.

Latrobe community, he learned all that a neighborhood could and should be and carried that into his creation of *Mister Rogers' Neighborhood*.

Like Mister Rogers, you have been shaped by the people around you—parents, grandparents, siblings, friends, neighbors, and colleagues. Whether intentionally or not, you carry different traits from them, even as you become the unique person God has created you to be. As you continue your journey, may you pick up a few of the characteristics of your giant as well.

JOURNAL

- As you explore the people who shaped your giant, what patterns or characteristics do you notice?

- What do you notice about the people who shaped you?

JOYFUL ACCEPTANCE OF GOD'S PLAN

Frances Chesterton was the wife of the famous British author and journalist G. K. Chesterton. Her life was one of quiet acceptance of God's plan for her. She had a rich faith, which she often expressed in her poetry.

As my giant, she taught me to be patient and persistent in my prayers, even when it seems as if my life plans are not working out or are falling apart. She also taught me to hope when things look hopeless. She taught me to be joyful amid sorrow.

Frances's loving support of her life partner, Gilbert, taught me that love is a decision to be made day after day, during good times and bad. That lesson can be applied to our spiritual lives as well, since on some days we feel God's intense love, while others are marked by wandering and doubt.

Most importantly, Frances's life encouraged me to do whatever I can to get closer to God. Her ability to ponder the meaning of circumstances deeply and search for joy in the everyday remains inspiring to me even now and helps me understand God.

—Nancy Carpentier Brown, author of *The Woman Who Was Chesterton* (Giant: Frances Chesterton, writer, 1869–1938)

SHAPED BY SUFFERING

Often out of periods of losing come the greatest strivings toward a new winning streak.

—FRED ROGERS, *You Are Special*

On *Mister Rogers' Neighborhood,* Mister Rogers's powerful messages of unconditional love and acceptance didn't come only from the nurturing of his parents, grandparents, and community, but they also came from the intense loneliness and rejection he suffered. An only child until age eleven, Fred had very few friends except the ones his mother chauffeured in for playdates. On one occasion, a few of his schoolmates chased him home from school and yelled, "Hey, Fat Freddy. We're going to get you!" Terrified, he ran to a neighbor's house and banged on the door until she let him in. When he told his parents what had happened, they told him the bullying would stop if he pretended he didn't care.

Through traumatic experiences like these, Fred absorbed the message that his peers would never look below the surface to see who he really was. He also learned that he couldn't always express his feelings. As a result, he often went to his piano and let his emotions pour out through his fingers. The hours of piano led to the creation of hundreds of songs that became tools for children to express their feelings and helped change the field of child psychology forever. One could say that Fred's difficulties during childhood helped ignite his life's passion of loving others not for what they were on the outside but for who they were on the inside.

Perhaps your childhood wasn't tied with a pretty bow of loving parents and grandparents, wealth, and an idyllic neighborhood but was instead marked by a dysfunctional family and significant scarring, loss, and pain. Maybe you've wondered if you can still make a positive contribution if your upbringing looked less like the sweet charm of *Mister Rogers' Neighborhood* and more like the chaotic mess of *The Simpsons*. Or you've worried that your traumas disqualify you from making a significant impact. Perhaps you've longed to have someone else's story or believed that the people who have made a real difference can't possibly have been as messed up as you think you are.

You might be surprised to learn that many of the greatest change makers in history have come from the messiest backgrounds. And in many cases, it was the hurdles they overcame that propelled them into leaving behind lasting legacies.

My own childhood was far from perfect. My mom was outgoing, warm, and generous. She enjoyed hosting parties and opening our home to those without family. Having experienced rejection in her own life, she was always looking for the one who was left out. My dad, a retired lieutenant colonel, managed multiple companies and one time even ran for mayor. But their marriage was fractured, and in the end, my mom had no choice but to leave. As for my dad, he started having more difficulty holding down jobs, began drinking more heavily, and eventually died of an alcohol overdose.

These earth-shattering events made indelible marks on my soul and dramatically shaped who I am today. I wish they'd never happened. But I also know that these early losses taught me to have more empathy for those who are suffering. While I inherited my parents' positive traits of hospitality and confidence, their failings also taught me the importance of perseverance and trust—not only in the career field but also in relationships and other areas of life.

You don't have to have a perfect upbringing to do something beautiful in this world. As was the case with Fred and perhaps the giant you've chosen, too, your greatest legacy will likely come from the melding of your euphoric moments and your scars.

JOURNAL

- How is God using your giant's scars to speak to you about your own?

INSPIRED TO SPEAK UP

Despite the stunning lengths Jesus went to in order to be our sympathetic, faithful, and merciful High Priest, I often struggle to see my life in His perfect one. In walking with Fannie Lou Hamer, I received the gift of learning from a woman who was a wife and mother, who lived in the same country as I do, and who allowed God to use every aspect of her life to bring His kingdom to her community.

Though we are separated by region, race, and political leanings, Fannie taught me how to be more gracious and humble toward those with different political and practical concerns. She taught me when to listen and when to speak up. Through her influence, the Spirit even nudged me to follow through on a conversation with the superintendent of our school system about a racist incident that had happened a few years ago in my classroom. Passionate about ensuring that our school becomes more intentional in keeping our commitment to deal with racism, I came away inspired to be more involved in the future.

—Kirstin Olson, high school teacher (Giant: Fannie Lou Hamer, women's/civil rights activist, 1917-77)

YOUR GIANT'S SPIRITUAL FORMATION

....

Spiritual formation is not something we do to ourselves or for ourselves, but something the Holy Spirit does in us as we seek God in the midst of ordinary life.

—EUGENE H. PETERSON, *Christ Plays in Ten Thousand Places*

Because of the incredible impact Fred had on the kingdom of God, you might think he had a dramatic conversion experience or perhaps some other life-altering event in his spiritual life. I certainly thought so, but when I dug deeper, the truth surprised me.

Raised in a Christian home by parents who were devoted to their local Presbyterian church, Fred was well versed in the tenets of hard work, responsibility, caring for others in the community, and serving God. His birthplace of Latrobe was the home of Saint Vincent Archabbey, the oldest Benedictine monastery in the United States. With these influences and his natural bent toward theology, he planned to attend seminary to become a Presbyterian minister.

But this plan changed during Easter break of his senior year. Flipping through the channels on his family's new television, he watched as a pie was thrown into a person's face and a roar of laughter erupted from the audience. Horrified by the display, he became gripped by what would become a lifelong passion to provide quality programming for young people.

In 1955, with a vision of reaching children through television, he enrolled in Pittsburgh Theological Seminary, where he met Dr. William Orr. Dr. Orr's life was a prime example of kindness and caring. He offered the staff and students his time, talents, and money. More than once, he returned from his lunch break without his coat, having given it to someone in need. Later, Fred referred to Dr. Orr as the person who came closest of anyone he knew to being a living saint.

Beyond surrounding himself with people who lived quiet lives of faith, Fred maintained his own consistent faith practices. Throughout his life, he faithfully woke up at five in the morning to read his Bible and pray. He was also a devoted member of his home church and was known to sit in the stillness of the archabbey on his way to work.

This description of Fred's spiritual formation might be surprising. Contrary to what one might think, he doesn't appear to have had any dramatic encounters with God or major shifts in his faith. He doesn't seem to have experienced a divine moment during any particular sermon when his ears were opened to the truth or he felt touched by God in a life-changing way.

The realization that Fred didn't have any dramatic conversion moment shocked me. Had I missed something? Or could some people's faith journeys simply be a gradual, day-by-day deepening relationship with God?

In my experience, going to Catholic school and attending church hadn't meant anything to my actual faith until I came to my own "eureka moment" and conversion. With this background, I often found myself judging others' relationships with God if they only performed the bare minimum of attending Sunday services. After all, if a person's faith didn't have fireworks, was it even real?

But as I explored more of Fred's faith journey, I realized I had been wrong. Wrong to assume I knew anyone's depth of faith simply from external appearances. Walking with Fred uncovered my own bias and provided a deeply humbling moment for me. It revealed a less-than-desirable way of thinking and showed me that my perspective needed to change.

Perhaps your giant's faith journey resembles Fred's. It might be similar to your own, or it might be surprising. One of the gifts of the giant journey is realizing that there are endless possibilities of how to come to know God and walk out a life of faith.

JOURNAL

- How does your giant's spiritual formation speak to you?

PILGRIMAGE PRINCIPLE

PAY ATTENTION TO YOUR EMOTIONS

The reality of naked trust is the life of a pilgrim who leaves what is nailed down, obvious, and secure, and walks into the unknown without any rational explanation to justify the decision or guarantee the future. Why? Because God has signaled the movement and offered it his presence and his promise.

—BRENNAN MANNING, *Ruthless Trust*

While enjoying a meal after a long day of walking the Camino trail, you find yourself drawn into conversation with fellow pilgrims. You trade answers to the common questions of name and origin, but then comes the deeper question of what brought you to the Camino. Maybe you were facing a big decision and needed some time away to figure out your priorities. Maybe you were drawn to the trail after hearing stories of transformation from previous pilgrims. Or maybe you felt a whisper of the Spirit or some other divine tug as you were going about your normal life.

On the Camino, every fellow traveler you encounter will have a unique story, but they will likely all share how their journey started with a spark. A moment when joy jumped inside them and they knew something significant had happened.

• • •

Any strong emotion is often a signal to pay attention. In fact, our strongest emotions can point in the direction God is leading us. Intense feelings of fear, happiness, or restlessness can act as flashing arrows meant to guide us to where God is calling us. These emotions are gifts at the crossroads of life, helping us figure out which way to go.

The Camino trail hasn't always been clearly marked. With only road signs and perhaps a map to follow, many pilgrims got lost along the trail over the years. Then, in 1984, Father Elías Valiña Sampedro, the parish priest of O Cebreiro in Galicia, Spain—guided by a divine spark—drove the five-hundred-mile trail across northern Spain. Using cans of yellow paint that he had stocked in his back seat, he painted the iconic yellow arrows, or *flechas,* to help keep pilgrims on course at tricky crossroads all the way to Santiago.*

Your emotions along the giant journey can act like flechas too. At difficult crossroads, imagine that God has gone before you with His yellow paint to guide you on the path to your sacred destination. Remain attuned to what excites you or troubles you on your journey and keep an eye out for flechas along the way.

JOURNAL

- Now that you're a quarter of the way down the trail, what are your strongest emotions?

- What topics or questions are you most excited about? What topics or questions are you most troubled by?

---

* "Yellow Arrows and Father Elias Valina," Caminofacil, accessed April 15, 2025, https://caminofacil.net/en/yellow-arrows-and-father-elias-valina/?utm_source=chatgpt.com.

MILE MARKER

The giant journey offers natural moments to pause at the side of the trail. Take time to do this at the end of each month.

FINAL STEPS ON THE TRAIL

- With this book and any other resources you used this month in hand, find a quiet time and place for reflection. Ask the Lord to open your eyes to anything He wants you to see as you review the Pilgrimage Principle and read through this month's journal prompts. Highlight anything that stands out to you and fill in any sections you might have skipped.
- After reading the Pilgrim Prayer below, take a few minutes to write your own prayer to God, thanking Him for how He perfectly designed you.
- Circle back to your month 3 trail guide and fill in any quotes, experiences, spiritual practices, or sticky points you haven't yet recorded.

REFLECTION

Take some time to reflect on the following questions as you wrap up the month. Your answers can be great indicators of what the Spirit might be leading you to focus on in the month ahead.

Summary: What direction did the Lord take you this month? Did your month go like you thought it would? Were there any unexpected leadings, twists, or turns?

Growth: In what areas of your life do you see growth or shifts in your thinking?

Excitement: When you think about your journey, what fills you with energy?

Challenges: What is bothering you? Do you have any unanswered questions or frustrations related to your journey?

PILGRIM PRAYER

Abba, thank You for orchestrating every part of my physical, spiritual, and emotional DNA and for perfectly shaping my spirit, soul, and body. Transform any weaknesses I have into superpowers for Your glory. Heal the parts of me that have been a source of shame. Knit together every part of me to bring life, beauty, and goodness to those around me. Oh Creator, give me eyes to see not only myself but also others as You do. Amen.

TRAVELOGUE

....

....

....

....

....

....

....

....

....

....

....

....

....

....

....

....

....

....

....

....

SEASON TWO

PERSEVERE

REVERBERATIONS

Whether en route to the physical or the interior Jerusalem, a pilgrim never walks alone. All need guides and companions for the journey . . . the great cloud of witnesses of the church eternal. . . . They bring their quirks, their foibles, and their full humanity to the journey. They meet us where we are, with our own foibles and our longing to find a way forward.

—LISA DEAM, *3000 Miles to Jesus*

STEPS ALONG THE TRAIL

As you begin season 2, change your focus from going wide to going deep. Instead of gathering information about your giant, become aware of how God is using your giant to speak specifically into your life. Use the focus points below as a guide:

☐ Pay attention to how your giant interacted with those around them, whether their family members, their colleagues, or the people they served. Consider how you might adopt any of your giant's practices as a way of relating more intentionally and practically to the people in your life this season.

☐ Look up any groups or organizations connected to your giant that are intriguing to you and learn more about them.

☐ Pick one topic, faith practice, quote, or godly characteristic your giant exhibited that has captivated or frustrated you and dig deeper into it this month.

☐ Remember that God has invited you on a unique journey. Don't worry if none of these ideas resonate with you. Just stay attuned to how the Spirit is guiding you.

☐ Complete the weekly journal prompts and the trail guide.

JOURNEY WITH FRED

Check out these resources if you're joining the giant journey with Mister Rogers:

- *The World According to Mister Rogers: Important Things to Remember* by Fred Rogers
- *You Are Special: Neighborly Words of Wisdom from Mister Rogers* by Fred Rogers (I recommend the audiobook!)

TRAIL GUIDE

Focus: What is your primary focus for this month? How is God directing your journey?

Media: What are you reading, watching, or listening to as you engage with your giant this month?

Quotes: What meaningful quotes would you like to remember from this month?

Experiences: What new places, activities, or events are you experiencing this month because of your giant?

Faith: In what ways has your giant drawn you closer to God this month? What spiritual practices have you engaged in as a result of your giant journey?

Sticky Points: What questions or topics might you want to explore more later?

RISING TO THE SURFACE

We know that in all things God works for the good of those who love him, who have been called according to his purpose.

—Romans 8:28

After walking with your giant for three months, you've probably learned quite a bit about their life and passions. You likely know the influences that shaped your giant and the people who formed their circle. You might even have a good grasp of their quirks and what made them tick. But amid all that information, maybe a certain aspect of your giant's life keeps rising to the surface of your mind. It might be your giant's relationship with a parent or mentor, a specific struggle or vice they wrestled with, or a deep longing they felt. Whatever it is, take notice—this is likely an area where the Spirit wants to work in you.

At this point of the journey, as you transition from going wide to going deep, rather than absorbing all the content you can get your hands on, try to choose only a few resources to ruminate on each month. As you explore them, pay attention to what jumps out at you and listen for the messages God might be whispering to you from your giant's life.

As I began my second season with Mister Rogers, I chose only two resources, because I knew I needed to leave plenty of space to grapple with the questions circling in my mind:

- How had Fred lived so simply and lovingly with his life as full as it was?

- How had this quirky man, with all his limitations and insecurities, made the impact he had?
- How had he honestly been able to say, "I like you just the way you are," so often? And why couldn't I celebrate that he said it—and lived it? What was buried in me that resisted or even felt threatened by this statement?

Having three months with Mister Rogers under my belt made me feel like I'd gained a lot of head knowledge about him. But understanding him was another matter. I didn't want to walk away from this journey unchanged, like the man in James 1:23–24, who looks at his face in a mirror only to walk away and forget what he looks like. While I'd learned about many admirable traits in Mister Rogers's life, now it was time to allow God to move below the surface and mold me into the person He had created me to be. It was only when I noticed some of these things repeatedly bubbling up and producing a reaction in me that I realized God was trying to get my attention.

You may be wrestling with things that God is bringing to the surface on your giant journey. Things that just won't leave you alone. As frustrating as this might be to hear, your time of wrestling might last for months or even years before you're able to receive the gift God wants to give you. But keep at it! These frustrations or unrealized promises are worth fighting through. They lead us to the golden nuggets that God places along our path to bring about lasting change and renewal.

JOURNAL

- As you reflect on your journey, what keeps rising up in your soul? What is nagging at you or feeling exciting? What experience, characteristic, quote, or habit of your giant just won't leave you alone?

A TREASURE HUNT WITH GOD

When I was assigned to walk with a spiritual giant, it felt like a waste of time. I had no idea who to choose.

Just after praying about it, I found a booklet mysteriously tucked into my suitcase. My son confessed that he had discovered a saint as weird as his mom and thought I might enjoy reading about her.

Not much was printed about Saint Faustina Kowalska, but I knew she was the one who had much to teach me.

Before being led to Faustina, I had been longing for companionship with someone whose experiences were a bit mystical. During my journey with Faustina, I learned I was not alone in my passion for Christ, which was like dousing a fire with gasoline. She saw herself as a simple delivery girl of God's message. I resonated with this and found it naturally flowing into my personal and work relationships.

Because I became so passionate about spiritual giants, I have been exuberantly teaching pastors and other church leaders about this great cloud of witnesses for the past five years. What started as a strange, unwelcome practice has become a regular part of my devotional life, a treasure hunt with God as my partner.

—Beth Klas, director of counseling (Giant: Faustina Kowalska, nun, 1905-38)

WEEK TWO

BLESSED RELIEF

....

I'll never forget the sense of wholeness I felt when I finally realized what I was—songwriter, telecommunicator, student of human development, language buff—but that all those things and more could be used in the service of children's healthy growing.

—FRED ROGERS, in *The Good Neighbor* by Maxwell King

Fred strongly believed in living a life of mission. He even carried a slip of paper in his wallet from his college days that read, "Life is for Service."* And he certainly lived it. During his television career, he wrote more than nine hundred episodes of *Mister Rogers' Neighborhood*, penned two hundred songs, and composed thirteen operas. He authored books and made speeches. He appeared in every episode of *Mister Rogers' Neighborhood*. When asked to describe himself, he said, "I'm a composer and a piano player, a writer and a television producer . . . almost by accident, a performer . . . a husband and a father. And I am a minister."[†]

All this while serving those around him and taking the time to love anyone who crossed his path.

Before I went on the giant journey with Mister Rogers, I imagined his life must have been way more pared down than mine. But then, as I explored the facets of his life, I learned the truth. And it struck me hard, challenging a limiting belief I hadn't known I'd been carrying.

---

* "'Life Is for Service:' The Words That Inspired Mister Rogers," From the Rollins Archives, https://blogs.rollins.edu/libraryarchives/2018/02/12/life-is-for-service-the-words-that-inspired-mister-rogers.

† Shea Tuttle, *Exactly as You Are: The Life and Faith of Mister Rogers* (Eerdmans, 2019), 3.

I'd been wrestling with the idea that living the life God wanted for me meant having an uncluttered calendar and lots of white space. Being a "master juggler" was something I tried to hide from the spiritual mentors I most respected, since I was convinced that I should know my top roles and limit them to two or three. In other words, if I was a wife, a mother, and my husband's business partner, I couldn't also be a spiritual director, retreat leader, and writer—despite feeling called to these pursuits.

Yet as I learned about all the roles Mister Rogers held and all the tasks he was responsible for, I was shocked. And then utterly relieved. This limitation I'd been living under was a rule I'd put on myself. Instead of agonizing over the number of roles I thought I was allowed to have, I realized that the important thing was to hold whatever roles I did have with grace. If I ever began to feel unbalanced, I could consider trimming something out. But until then, I could follow all these passions where I felt God's leading. Through my journey with Fred, God opened my eyes to wondrous and life-giving freedom.

It might be easy to believe that our giants never struggled with feeling out of balance or having bulging calendars. The truth is, they lived not perfectly but prayerfully—doing the best they could, just like we can.

If you ever feel conflicted about your schedule or some other facet of your life, take a good look at your giant and know that you are in good company. It is possible to live in the twenty-first century with our full calendars and broad responsibilities and still be in the center of God's will. We're all human, and if we can give grace to one another, we can certainly give it to ourselves as well.

JOURNAL

- As a result of walking with your giant, what relief or grace have you experienced for something you wrestle with?

HEALING OINTMENT

My hunch is that anyone who has ever been able to sustain good work has had at least one person—and often many—who have believed in him or her. We just don't get to be competent human beings without a lot of different investments from others.

—FRED ROGERS, *You Are Special*

Fred worked hard at his friendships. Though people might think that intimate friendship flowed naturally for him, the truth is that he prepared for, took notes about, and kept files on his important relationships. Compelled by his profound reverence for every sacred soul, he wanted to carefully steward every opportunity to extend and receive friendship.

While I listened to a few minutes of an interview about Fred, I thought of my friend Lisa. She felt torn about the pace of her life. In addition to being a devoted hospice nurse, she and her husband pastor a small but vibrant church. She is also away from home two or three days a week to help her daughters-in-law care for their young families. As a result, her walk of faith doesn't always include sipping a steaming cup of coffee during her unhurried morning quiet time. Instead, as she drives to wherever her day takes her, she pops in a CD or audiobook and enjoys time with the Lord as the miles whiz by. Her sanctuary looks very different from what most would call normal. But this is the life that God has given her. She is living at the pace of love.

When I learned about all the hats Fred wore so well and the intentionality he carried into his relationships despite his full life, I couldn't wait to call Lisa. Even if her life remained as full as ever—as Fred's did—she could perhaps find peace in knowing that she was walking in the center of God's will.

As you walk the trail with your giant, you might discover a treasure from God that's meant not just for you but for other pilgrims as well. Something you learn may free another traveler of pain or better equip them for their own journey. That's what being friends—and fellow pilgrims—is all about.

JOURNAL

- What have you learned on your giant journey that could be a revelation or good news to someone else?

CHALLENGES EVEN IN A FAITHFUL LIFE

Rembrandt van Rijn is one of those artists who is so iconic that we know him by his first name. Throughout his career, he created hundreds of paintings, prints, and drawings that illustrate key moments from biblical stories. In studying the connections between art and the spiritual life, I have returned to his work again and again.

Like many other artists, Rembrandt experienced ups and downs and, after great initial acclaim, struggled for recognition in his later years. He suffered the death of his beloved wife and a treasured son, as well as financial challenges that caused him to lose virtually everything. But to the end, he focused most of his talent on bringing to life the biblical stories that had guided him along his spiritual path.

His work has been a continuing inspiration to me, and his life a reminder that even a faithful life will have its challenges—but that, in our darkest hours, we can always return to the embrace of the God who loves us.

—Terry Glaspey, author of *75 Masterpieces Every Christian Should Know*, professor at Northwind Theological Seminary (Giant: Rembrandt van Rijn, artist, 1606–69)

WHEN OUR GIANTS CHALLENGE US

··

When we love a person, we accept him or her exactly as is: the lovely with the unlovely, the strong along with the fearful, the true mixed in with the façade, and of course, the only way we can do it is by accepting ourselves that way.

—FRED ROGERS, *You Are Special*

On your giant journey—whether it's alongside Mister Rogers or someone else—you have likely come across statements, beliefs, or practices in your giant's life that give you pause. You might disagree with them entirely or struggle to accept them as true for yourself. Make a note of these areas of struggle whenever you stumble upon them. These may be the very things that spark transformation.

In my journey with Fred, I experienced a severe internal battle over one of his most well-known statements: "I like you just the way you are." Those words haunted me. I wanted to like or even love people just the way they were, but was that even possible? He couldn't have honestly meant *all* of a person—their gifts *and* their flaws—when he said that. But what if he did? Was it possible to love someone like that? Could *I* do that?

For years, I've struggled to love my mom exactly the way she is because of the destructive choices she repeatedly makes. Christ is the Savior and Redeemer of her life, but she's never been able to overcome her tendency toward unhealthy relationships with men. It's been painful to watch her suffer each time another man hurts or disappoints her.

Her issues with men began early. She was an only child born to a harsh father who wanted a son. She then married her high school sweetheart only to be divorced within ten years. Soon after, looking for a strong man that she could feel safe with, she fell in love with and married my dad, a lieutenant colonel in the army. Things were good for the first few years, but then in the brokenness of PTSD, his life spiraled out of control and he overdrank one night to the point that it killed him. And there was my mom, widowed at age forty-two and torn to pieces by another broken relationship.

Jesus promises He will heal us. Just as He told the woman at the well, who was searching for a man to fill the holes in her heart, our thirst can be quenched only by Him (John 4:13–14). He will heal the broken places in each of us if we let Him.

And yet sometimes we can't. Sometimes we won't. As humans, we don't always do things perfectly. We make mistakes. But is it possible to love one another despite our mistakes, even if they are ongoing? The people around us are extraordinary in countless ways. Do we expect or even demand perfection from them? Or do we allow them to be human?

François Clemmons, the actor who played the police officer on *Mister Rogers' Neighborhood,* was a gay man—a lifestyle that was a contradiction of Fred's biblical theology. But over the years, Fred showed François genuine love and acceptance. After Fred's death, François told journalists about one day during taping when Fred was reciting, "I like you just the way you are." As he said it, he looked directly across the studio at François, communicating in a way they both understood that he meant every word.

What if we could love like that? Embracing others even while wanting something better for them? What if we could look at one another and say, "I like you just the way you are," and truly mean it? After all, that's what God does for us.

JOURNAL

- What quote from your giant's life has made a significant impact on you?

PILGRIMAGE PRINCIPLE

CHOOSE LESS

Contentment is not the fulfillment of what you want, but the realization of how much you already have.

—Author Unknown

On day 12 of your thirty-five-day trek along the Camino, you open your eyes to see your fellow travelers milling around the *albergue* (the dormitory-style pilgrim hostel) you arrived at the night before. As you sit up and stretch, some pilgrims head to the showers while others pack up their gear so they can get ahead of the heat and on the trail before daylight. Many of these people have become your "Camino family." It feels like you've known them all your life, and you can already see yourself walking the whole trail together and celebrating when you reach Santiago.

But even as you imagine that possible end to the journey, a different longing stirs in you. As you rub your pleasantly sore muscles and reflect on all the beautiful towns and churches you've encountered so far— every one of them a masterpiece—you realize you need a day to process. A day to sit and journal, even if it means being separated from your Camino family. A day to be quiet and reflect instead of being pumped with adrenaline or conversing with pilgrims from every country. You realize you don't want to absorb anything else right now but instead want to chew on what you've already experienced. Even if you don't meet up with your little Camino family again, finish "on time," or make it to Santiago with everyone else, you know the right thing for you is to stay back and savor.

• • •

Sometimes the best thing is not turning up the gas but turning it down. The same is true for your giant journey. There will be times when you're full of enthusiasm, excited to read and study, and eager to plunge into new territory. But then there will be other times when what you need is not to take in more but to take a closer look at what you already have.

You might worry that taking a month to process will keep you from covering every topic or question you hoped to explore. Yet choosing less often delivers more. You may have dreams and plans, but only God knows the things that are truly important on your journey. So stay attuned to the Spirit's direction for your path, discerning if you should go forward or pause and what you should focus on next. You may not keep pace with those around you or reach all the milestones you mapped out ahead of time, but you can trust that God will lead you to what your heart is truly longing for.

JOURNAL

- What do you feel the Spirit saying to you about your journey at this stage?

- Is the month ahead a good time to take in more or savor what you've already received?

MILE MARKER

The giant journey offers natural moments to pause at the side of the trail. Take time to do this at the end of each month.

FINAL STEPS ON THE TRAIL

....

- With this book and any other resources you used this month in hand, go somewhere different than you normally would to reflect and pray. Treat yourself to a latte at your favorite coffee shop or sit in the sunshine at the park. Ask God to open your ears to hear His voice as you review the Pilgrimage Principle, read through your notes, and highlight anything that stands out to you.
- Before completing the reflection questions, take fifteen minutes to journal about the ideas that have been stirring in you during your journey this month. Then take a few minutes to give thanks, bring God your questions, and talk to Him about the things that are troubling or exciting you.
- Circle back to the trail guide and fill in any quotes, experiences, spiritual practices, or sticky points you haven't yet recorded.

REFLECTION

Take some time to reflect on the following questions as you wrap up the month. Your answers can be great indicators of what the Spirit might be leading you to focus on in the month ahead.

Summary: What direction did the Lord take you this month? Did your month go like you thought it would? Were there any unexpected leadings, twists, or turns?

Growth: In what areas of your life do you see growth or shifts in your thinking?

Excitement: When you think about your journey, what fills you with energy?

Challenges: What is bothering you? Do you have any unanswered questions or frustrations related to your journey?

PILGRIM PRAYER

Faithful Counselor, the one who knows all mysteries and is just waiting for me to ask, I come to You today, thankful for Your work in my life. Lord, I can't comprehend Your love for me and that as great as Your plan for the universe is, nothing gives You more joy than when I ask You to guide me. Help me remain faithful to my small part. Open my eyes and my ears. Amen.

TRAVELOGUE

SAVOR THE EXPERIENCE

The biggest lesson I learned on the Camino was that I needed to slow down. . . . I discovered during my days as a pilgrim that I could not be at peace unless I walked in a relaxed manner both internally and externally. . . . Undoubtedly, it will take a lifetime for me to fully learn the lesson of walking in a relaxed manner.

—JOYCE RUPP, *Walk in a Relaxed Manner*

STEPS ALONG THE TRAIL

One of the most powerful lessons we can learn from our giants is how they practiced knowing, loving, and walking with God. With that in mind, here are a few possible focus points for the month ahead:

☐ Dig deeper into your giant's spiritual life. Discover how their relationship with God came alive and consider what their lifelong relationship with Him looked like.

☐ Explore one or more spiritual practices (prayer, hymns, evangelism, Bible study, cultural faith traditions, silence, nature, music, etc.) that were significant in your giant's walk with God and be open to how God might use them to deepen your relationship with Him.

☐ Listen to God's leading on how you should explore this practice, whether by ordering a book or another resource to learn more about it or by participating in the practice in a specific way.

☐ Invite a friend to join you in exploring the practice this month to keep you accountable.

☐ Remember that God has invited you on a unique journey. Don't worry if none of these ideas resonate with you. Just stay attuned to how the Spirit is guiding you.

☐ Complete the weekly journal prompts and the trail guide.

 ## JOURNEY WITH FRED

Check out these resources if you're joining the giant journey with Mister Rogers:

- *Exactly as You Are: The Life and Faith of Mister Rogers* by Shea Tuttle
- *Mister Rogers' Neighborhood: It's a Beautiful Day Collection,* PBS

TRAIL GUIDE

Focus: What is your primary focus for this month? How is God directing your journey?

Media: What are you reading, watching, or listening to as you engage with your giant this month?

Quotes: What meaningful quotes would you like to remember from this month?

Experiences: What new places, activities, or events are you experiencing this month because of your giant?

Faith: In what ways has your giant drawn you closer to God this month? What spiritual practices have you engaged in as a result of your giant journey?

Sticky Points: What questions or topics might you want to explore more later?

YOUR GIANT'S STRONGEST SPIRITUAL PRACTICE

....

> What can we do to encourage people to have more quiet in their lives, more silence? Real revelation comes through silence.
>
> —FRED ROGERS, "Remembering Mister Rogers,"
> interview with Charlie Rose

After four months of walking with your giant—reading about their life, listening to podcasts, jotting down notes, and journaling—take a minute to gauge your appetite. If you're still feeling hungry to learn more, consider diving into a new resource. But if you're feeling filled to the brim or overwhelmed by the amount of information you've absorbed already, God may be leading you to focus intentionally on less. One way you can do that is by spending the month ahead leaning into a single spiritual practice of your giant that most appeals to you.

Usually, I'm never happier than when I have a book in my hand or when I'm listening to a podcast, but as I headed into month 5 with Fred, I realized I wanted the input to stop. While praying about my month's focus, I felt God reminding me about Mister Rogers's spiritual practice of silence, the first divine thread that had tugged me near the beginning of the journey. God had been slowly weaving this practice into my life over the past decade, ever since I'd attended my first silent retreat. Since then, I'd participated in numerous day retreats but had never spent a whole weekend in silence with God. I had no idea what it would be like to attend a silent retreat with a group. Though the idea of such an endeavor felt completely foreign and even a little frightening, I was certain that was the practice God was inviting me to try.

To my relief, the weekend of silence turned out to be filled with tears, joy, and a greater sense of God's love than I'd ever known. Afterward, I could barely come up with an answer when people asked, "So, how was it?" All I knew was that the experience had birthed in me a desire to go on a silent retreat every year and to take others with me so they could appreciate the wonder of the practice too.

Perhaps your giant was an advocate of silence as well. If that is the case or if you're walking with Mister Rogers with me, consider booking a silent retreat for yourself. Or if that feels impossible with your current schedule or life stage, try to think of other ways you can escape from the noise—even for a few hours—to enjoy silence with God. You could go on a walk in your neighborhood, sit in a park or forest, or take a long bath without listening to music or anything else. You could even adjust your commute by driving with the stereo off and spending the time in silence with God instead.

If your giant followed some other spiritual practice, challenge yourself to try it—especially if it's one you don't already regularly engage in. Perhaps they often fasted or dedicated certain parts of their week to serving others. Or maybe they began each morning with a specific prayer practice. Whatever you decide to do, remember to seek the Spirit's guidance and to enjoy the journey as you follow the path God has prepared for you.

JOURNAL

- What spiritual practice that your giant followed are you drawn to try yourself?

WEEK TWO

BEING A DISCIPLE TAKES DISCIPLINE

....

You rarely have time for everything . . . so you need to make choices.
And hopefully your choices can come from a deep sense of who you
are.

—FRED ROGERS, *The World According to Mister Rogers*

One of the most powerful gifts of the giant journey is the lessons
God reveals to you through your giant's spiritual practices.
This isn't to say learning them is easy. It will often require
prayerful discipline and intentional effort on your part if you are truly
going to let these lessons take root in your heart and life. But the payoff—
eventual transformation—is worth it.

Fred's wife, Joanne, and Hedda Sharapan, a key staff member who
worked closely with him on *Mister Rogers' Neighborhood* and at Fred
Rogers Productions, consistently reminded people that it was not some
innate godliness that made Fred into the person he was but disciplined
hard work. "Just don't make Fred into a saint," Joanne would say. "If
you make him out to be a saint, people might not know how hard he
worked." Hedda added, "They'll think he's some otherworldly
creature."* The truth is, Fred was very much human—just one who
lived with determined purpose and discipline. From his health and professional life to his relationship with God and intentional presence with
others, he lived like a runner, always keeping the prize before him.

---

* Jeanne Marie Laskas, "The Mister Rogers No One Saw," *New York Times Magazine*, No-
vember 19, 2019, www.nytimes.com/2019/11/19/magazine/mr-rogers.html.

As I followed God's leading to go deeper into Fred's spiritual practice of silence, I quickly realized that it required a lot of discipline to resist the urge to turn on music, an audiobook, or a podcast. Choosing silence definitely didn't feel natural, especially during tasks that were usually accompanied by background noise. But as I remained consistent with the practice, I noticed small changes slowly working their way into my heart.

One day, while I painted in silence, a conversation I'd had with a friend a few days earlier floated through my mind. I'd been telling her about my new church and joked that I was surprised to like it because I'd been sure it would be full of "rednecks." Even though my friend hadn't said anything at the time, I felt God revealing to me during my silent painting session how unkind my statement had been. Those hadn't been words of love. Nor had they been a reflection of the person God had created me to be. Embarrassed by my uncaring attitude and thoughtless words, I felt nudged to repent. Because I'd obeyed the Lord's leading to prioritize silence, my ears weren't clogged with other noise and I was able to hear His voice.

For you, the giant journey may require discipline in another area. Perhaps other activities are providing unnecessary distractions that are keeping you from pursuing your walk with God alongside your giant. Or maybe boredom or restlessness is trying to lure you away from the journey altogether.

I urge you to press on, holding tight to the hope of how God will shape you if you persevere. Being a disciple takes discipline. The Lord has called you to this journey, and it's the daily, weekly, and monthly steps of obedience that will bring about your transformation.

JOURNAL

- How are you struggling to persevere in following the guidance the Spirit has given you this month?

A TWENTY-FIVE-YEAR FRIENDSHIP

I met Francis de Sales through his writing during my pastoral ministry studies more than twenty-five years ago. From that first meeting, he felt like a kindred spirit. I resonated with his Jesus-centered, practical spirituality, the gentleness with which he approached everything and everyone, and his constant exhortation to "live Jesus."

Francis taught me to pray with my "affections," bringing my feelings honestly before God. As someone who is centered on my thoughts and often ignores my emotions, I can't overstate the importance of this shift in embracing my own and others' humanity.

He reminded me often of God's loving gaze and that one's relationship with Him is a love affair. His example of pouring himself out for others' needs has made me think twice when I am tempted to pull back and conserve my energy for myself.

He will always be a spiritual mentor to me. I live in gratitude for what he taught me, and I am still learning from his writing.

—Kathy Hasty, pediatric physical therapist
(Giant: Francis de Sales, bishop, writer, 1567–1622)

HUMILITY IS SHOWING UP

Doing "the best we can" may still fall short of what we would like . . .
but life isn't perfect . . . and doing what we can with what we have is
the most we should expect of ourselves or anyone else.

—FRED ROGERS, *The World According to Mister Rogers*

In the thirty years that *Mister Rogers' Neighborhood* aired on television, every episode began in the same way: Mister Rogers would open the door to his home, walk inside, smile, and sing, "It's a beautiful day in the neighborhood. It's a beautiful day to be neighbors. Would you be mine? Could you be mine? Won't you be my neighbor?" He would put on his comfy sweater and change into his sneakers. Then, after welcoming viewers into his living room, he would show his audience a gadget he had brought with him and explain how it worked. After that, the little trolley would enter the set behind him, and he would take the audience to the Neighborhood of Make-Believe, where the puppets performed skits with actors dressed up in costumes.

For some, the show might be a little painful to watch. The trolley jerks along the tracks. The skits are corny. Grown men and women are dressed up like dogs and parrots. Mister Rogers doesn't come across as cool or charismatic.

But in every episode, he was 100 percent love, no matter how unpolished his delivery. He wasn't worried about his reputation. He didn't refuse to be taped until he became a more impressive speaker. With five episodes to write, produce, and act in every week, he had to let the show go out to viewers whether or not he felt it was the best reflection of himself.

According to what was popular at the time, the show wasn't that good. But Mister Rogers gave what he had. He wrote the programs and then walked onstage, even though he never wanted to be the one on camera. He would have preferred to be behind the scenes, playing the music and orchestrating the puppets. But when the station manager told him they needed him as the star of the show, he rose to the challenge despite not feeling qualified.

You may resonate with that experience of imposter syndrome. You might worry that others are better equipped to fulfill your roles. You might wake up several days a week and wonder what you're even doing. Believe me: I know the feeling.

As a new spiritual director, I go into most meetings with a breath and a prayer, since I often feel like I don't know what I'm doing. During a recent appointment, I felt led to slowly read a passage of Scripture three times while the directee sat with her eyes closed, opening herself to God. My reading wasn't smooth. My instructions weren't the clearest. My pauses between readings were inconsistent. But when I looked up after the final reading, I saw tears streaming down her cheeks. God had met her.

The truth is, we are never going to feel completely prepared to do every task or handle every responsibility. But that's okay. The important thing is to be faithfully present, to show up consistently in places where we don't have it all together, and to offer our best as we do the work God has called us to.

Remember, humility is showing up whether we have everything down or not. We must let go of perfectionism and give what we have. God will do the rest.

JOURNAL

- How has your giant encouraged you to show up and do what God has called you to?

PRIORITIZING MY SPIRITUAL JOURNEY

Julian of Norwich—Norwich being a small town in England twenty minutes from where I lived between the ages of one and four—became my spiritual giant. Her choice to confine her life to one small room made a profound impact on me.

COVID ground our lives to a halt. The first sermon I preached during the quarantine was entitled "Two Windows" and focused on how one window of Julian's cubicle looked into the church and the other allowed her contact with the village. She couldn't see out, but she could hear people as they came to that window for spiritual direction. Her other window allowed her to see the communion elements and to derive spiritual nourishment from the congregation. She couldn't enjoy their embraces. Hearing their voices needed to suffice. So similar to how our world felt during the early stages of the pandemic.

I'm struck by the chosen sparseness of her life, which challenges me to prioritize my spiritual journey and not get caught up in materialism. Living in increasingly tumultuous times, just as she did facing the Black Death and the Hundred Years' War, I am continually strengthened by her famous quote, "All shall be well, and all shall be well, and all manner of things shall be well."

—Laurie TenHave-Chapman, minister, hospice grief chaplain,
PreachingLife.net (Giant: Julian of Norwich,
anchoress, mystic, ca. 1342-1416)

HEALING WHERE YOU NEED IT MOST

....

> Whenever I hear someone speak of privacy, I find myself thinking once again how real and deep the need for such times is for all human beings . . . at all ages.
>
> —FRED ROGERS, *The World According to Mister Rogers*

Fred seemed like he was from a different world. Even as culture insisted that one's purpose could be found only in more people, information, travel, and accomplishment, he became a voice to all ages saying that our greatest fulfillment would be not in hustling "out there" but in drawing back and waiting on God. As I followed his spiritual practice of spending time in solitude and silence, God opened the door to parts of the abundant life that had been eluding me.

The silent retreat I was leading that year was supposed to be a time of rest, renewal, and simplicity. A much-needed space in the middle of a busy season where I could take a breath and reconnect with God, others, and myself. But thanks to the fears and insecurities created by childhood wounds, "myself" was getting in the way. As the leader and keynote speaker, I was feeling the internal pressure to perform and to be perfectly polished. With that weight pressing down on me, I had stuffed my suitcase full of books, commentaries, and journals. My plan was to fight that inner voice saying "Not good enough" by doing everything in my power to ensure the retreat went off without a hitch. I was open to the movement of the Spirit's power, too, but in my anxiety, I wanted to prepare for every eventuality—just in case.

Thankfully, God had a better plan.

During that first day, every time I tried to open a book or listen to a podcast, I couldn't. Instead, I felt God calling me to spend the time in silence—cutting off all voices except His and my own. Reluctantly, I listened. And then, to my complete amazement, I sensed the fullness of God's presence passing by me on the third day of silence. In that moment, He opened my eyes to the fear that had been churning in my gut since childhood, fear that my past had damaged and disqualified me. Shattering these lies, God revealed His plan to heal me. He let me know that I was enough, that my voice mattered, and that I could rest in being who He had created me to be. Just like that, I felt that fear dissolve. By listening to the Spirit's leading to spend the time in silence, I experienced a profound sense of peace and a miraculous healing from a wound I had been carrying for years.

Whether you're walking with Mister Rogers or another giant on this journey, God led you to that person for a reason. He knows where you most need healing or freedom. He knows the spiritual practices that will put you in a position to finally receive all He has been longing to give you. Maybe you've been needing to find a sense of direction, purpose, or belonging. Maybe you weren't sure what you needed when you began this journey, but God has been using your giant to reveal the hidden longings or scars in your heart. Listen to His voice and follow His leading so that you are open to those breakthroughs. When you do, you can trust He is going to bring transformation and healing.

JOURNAL

- As you go deeper into one of your giant's spiritual practices, what do you notice the Lord doing in your life?

PILGRIMAGE PRINCIPLE

WIDEN YOUR CIRCLE

....

Each of us has a camino, a road of life. This road allows us access to the spiritual richness of those who traveled before us and those who travel with us now. . . . These people of faith are our teachers and catalysts of inspiration.

—JOYCE RUPP, *Walk in a Relaxed Manner*

After a beautiful day's walk on the Camino, you arrive at the albergue and drop off your pack. Sore and dusty from all the miles you traveled today, you decide to take a long, hot shower. You tell your traveling companions you'll meet them later for dinner, and they mention a special restaurant they've picked out and let you know that another friend will be joining the group—someone who has walked the Camino before and has much wisdom to offer. Excited by the prospect, you head off to the showers and begin to imagine who this pilgrim might be and what you might learn from them.

• • •

After months of walking only with Mister Rogers, I knew it was time to meet one of the people who had profoundly shaped him into who he was—his dear friend and spiritual mentor, author and theologian Henri Nouwen. I had admired Nouwen for a long time and had been chomping at the bit to delve into his life. But every time I tried to write him into my monthly focus section, I could feel the Spirit saying, "Not yet." There was still more to learn from Mister Rogers. Finally, as I neared the year's halfway point, I could sense that it was time to welcome Henri Nouwen to the journey.

In human relationships, one plus one never just equals two. Each person is a combination of the people they encounter throughout their lives.

From the moment a baby is born and set in their mother's arms, they will never be just one again. Their mother has begun to shape them—then their father, siblings, and friends will do the same. The multiplication has started.

The same is true of the giant journey. Whenever your giant "introduces" you to those who influenced them, you gain the opportunity to be shaped not just by one giant but by many. So don't be surprised if God speaks to you not only through your own giant but also through their giants as well!

JOURNAL

- Which significant mentors, friends, or other influences in your giant's life are you drawn to?

MILE MARKER

The giant journey offers natural moments to pause at the side of the trail. Take time to do this at the end of each month.

FINAL STEPS ON THE TRAIL

- By this time, you're probably comfortable with your Mile Markers. However, the danger with being comfortable is that you may be tempted to drift into autopilot, so remember to shake things up a bit when you can!
- Find a quiet time and place and ask the Lord to open your heart to a revelation He wants to use to shape you. As an interesting twist, after reading through your notes with a highlighter and filling in any sections you've missed, write a letter to God or email to a friend about what the Lord has been doing in your life through this journey. Notice what comes to the surface.

REFLECTION

....

Take some time to reflect on the following questions as you wrap up the month. Your answers can be great indicators of what the Spirit might be leading you to focus on in the month ahead.

Summary: What direction did the Lord take you this month? Did your month go like you thought it would? Were there any unexpected leadings, twists, or turns?

Growth: In what areas of your life do you see growth or shifts in your thinking?

Excitement: When you think about your journey, what fills you with energy?

Challenges: What is bothering you? Do you have any unanswered questions or frustrations related to your journey?

PILGRIM PRAYER

Holy Spirit, thank You for always guiding me to understand more of who You are and for leading me into new practices to help me know You better. Whenever I try to box You in or think that I can grow closer to You only in certain ways, please keep me from growing rigid or complacent and blow the doors wide open with something brand new. Oh Spirit, help me stay curious and receptive. Amen.

TRAVELOGUE

SECONDARY COMPANIONS

We desperately need wise spiritual guides to point out the way, to tell us to keep moving, to put a hand on our shoulder and tell us that the darkness will not consume us, to tell us that God's peculiar ways are signals of grace, and that we must just wait and see.

—WINN COLLIER, *Let God*

STEPS ALONG THE TRAIL

One of the great benefits of walking with a giant is that you have the privilege to learn not only from them but also from those they were connected to, such as their mentors, pastors, or literary heroes. With that in mind, consider this focus point for the month ahead:

☐ Receive from one of your giant's giants: From the list of your giant's significant influences that you jotted down last month, select the one you are most drawn to learn from and decide what resources or experiences you will use to do that.

☐ Remember that God has invited you on a unique journey. Don't worry if this idea doesn't resonate with you. Just stay attuned to how the Spirit is guiding you.

☐ Complete the weekly journal prompts and the trail guide.

 ## JOURNEY WITH FRED

Check out these resources if you're joining the giant journey with Mister Rogers:
- *Adam: God's Beloved* by Henri Nouwen
- *Henri Nouwen: Writings Selected with an Introduction* by Robert A. Jonas

TRAIL GUIDE

Focus: What is your primary focus for this month? How is God directing your journey?

Media: What are you reading, watching, or listening to as you engage with your giant this month?

Quotes: What meaningful quotes would you like to remember from this month?

Experiences: What new places, activities, or events are you experiencing this month because of your giant?

Faith: In what ways has your giant drawn you closer to God this month? What spiritual practices have you engaged in as a result of your giant journey?

Sticky Points: What questions or topics might you want to explore more later?

DIVINE MULTIPLICATION

> Take a minute to think of at least one person who helped you to become who you are *inside* today. . . . Just one minute . . . one minute to think of those who have made a real difference in your life.
>
> —FRED ROGERS, *You Are Special*

Throughout his life, Mister Rogers shared that none of us becomes who we are without many other "neighbors" who pour their love and gifts into us. He glowingly talked about the many "neighbors" who shaped him:

- The people who were part of his childhood: his grandfather; neighbor Mama Bell, whose porch door was always open to visitors; and Jim Stumbaugh, a high school friend.
- The strong influences he was fortunate to meet in person: Yo-Yo Ma, internationally renowned cellist; Bo Lozoff, co-founder of Human Kindness Foundation; and Dr. Benjamin Spock, acclaimed pediatrician and author of *The Common Sense Book of Baby and Child Care.*
- Those who shaped him from a distance: Mahatma Gandhi, freedom activist; Albert Schweitzer, Nobel Peace Prize winner; and Jane Addams, peace advocate.
- Those who were intimate mentors: chief among them, Henri Nouwen, world-renowned priest, theologian, and friend.

Fred met Henri at his Harvard home through a mutual friend who, knowing they both had a passion for spirituality and psychology, felt they would get along famously. He was right. Kindred spirits from their first meeting, they then formed a lifelong friendship of meeting in person, talking on the phone, and exchanging letters. Gentle souls, they shared an empathy for others and were passionate activists.

Often when Henri phoned Fred, he would speak so quickly that Fred could barely keep up. After sharing about the part of the world he happened to be in at the moment, Henri would quickly come to the point of his call and ask Fred, "How are you?" He cared deeply for Fred, and since Fred was often the one pouring himself out for others, he needed those people in his life who would care for him. In a tribute to Henri, Fred said, "Each morning I pray for my family and my friends—by name. When I come to Henri's name, I look at his photo on the back of his 'Adam' book, and I put my fingers on his sweater and I say, 'Thank you.' "*

After Henri died, Fred described him as the one who helped him "grow into a thoughtful person who cares about the essentials of life."† One of the practices Fred learned from Henri was the practice of silence, which then became one of the greatest gifts Fred offered to the children and adults he influenced. As he explained it, "Henri's death has confirmed for me the enormous power of silence. Even though most of the world knows Henri best by his words, I've come to recognize his deepest respect for the still, small voice among the quiet of eternity. That's what continues to inspire me."‡

As you walk with your giant, you may encounter many people who inspired them and who call out to you as they called out to your giant. For me, as I learned about those who had shaped Fred, I knew many of them could have much to teach me, but I was especially drawn to Henri. If you sense a similar leading, trust this as a nudge from the Spirit. God may have other gifts for you in the lives of your giant's giants. As you

---

* Christopher de Vinck, ed., *Nouwen Then: Personal Reflections on Henri* (Zondervan, 1999), 77, 78.

† Melissa Guerrero, "Mister Rogers's Surprising Ties with Catholicism," EpicPew, accessed March 7, 2025, https://epicpew.com/mister-rogerss-surprising-ties-with-catholicism.

‡ De Vinck, ed., *Nouwen Then*, 77.

listen to the Spirit's guidance and decide which mentor of your giant you might like to invite along on the trail, may you experience a divine multiplication of the journey!

JOURNAL

- Who in your giant's life do you feel called to learn from? What characteristic of one of your giant's giants is intriguing to you? Why?

A LIFE IN SERVICE OF OTHERS

For years, I have been drawn to amazing things in creation. When I discovered leprosy surgeon Paul Brand's book *Fearfully and Wonderfully Made,* I was hooked! I had no idea the effect that book would have on me—giving me not only a deeper awe for our bodies but also an awareness of a truly humble man, who was utterly devoted to God and gave his life for others.

As I go about my daily life, I think about Brand's love for God and how he gave his life to the revolutionary work of serving the forgotten people suffering from leprosy in India—people that no one, not even the medical community, dared go near.

Brand has led me closer to God and His Son, Jesus, and has introduced me to author and theologian Philip Yancey, whose writing I am drawn to know better. He inspires me to see each person as valuable no matter how insignificant society has deemed them, and he has increased my longing to share about God's amazing creation and to give my life in service to others. Both are passions that will continue to find expression in my life through the years ahead.

—Ellen Landreth, business owner, TheSantaCouple.com (Giant: Paul Brand, leprosy surgeon, writer, 1914-2003)

HELP IN FINDING OUR WAY

I do love being a grandfather, and I wonder if it wasn't because my grandfather McFeely loved me so much.

—FRED ROGERS, *The World According to Mister Rogers*

Henri Nouwen was a Dutch priest, award-winning writer, and renowned theology professor who spent much of his life teaching at Notre Dame, Yale, and Harvard. But despite his many significant accomplishments, Henri became restless. He felt an emptiness, a need for home, and a longing for neighbors who knew and loved him.

That longing eventually took him to L'Arche, a community for the disabled in Ontario, Canada, where he served as the primary caregiver for one of the neediest residents, a profoundly disabled man named Adam. During his time there, Henri dressed, shaved, and fed Adam. He supported each of Adam's steps from behind and remained by his side through his frequent seizures. Even though Adam could never speak, they communicated more deeply than words could express. It seems that Henri learned more about God and the essence of life from that year alone than from the rest of his career.

In the final year of his life, Henri endeavored to do what he considered would be his greatest work: to write a modern translation of the Apostle's Creed, one of the foundations of the Christian faith. He wrestled with how to put these great truths into words, but no matter how hard he tried, the translation wouldn't come together.

Then, unexpectedly, Adam died. In Henri's grief as he reflected on this tremendous man, he realized that the best illustration of the Christian faith was not a translation of the Apostle's Creed; it was the choice to care for the least of these, in community, through the simplest acts of love—one human being to another.

Mister Rogers's life was a powerful illustration of loving those closest to him and being fully present with them. In addition to becoming one of America's favorite and most caring neighbors on television, he was also a devoted husband, a faithful friend, and a beloved father and grandfather. He knew that none of the public roles he had would matter if he wasn't able to show love in his most intimate ones.

Like Fred's, much of my life has revolved around the intimate role of being a parent. But after raising six children and watching each of them head off on their own adventures, I entered the empty-nest years eager to explore roles I hadn't been able to previously. My husband and I launched a retreat center. I became a spiritual director, started leading retreats, and began writing.

Then I became a grandmother.

To my horror and dismay, my initial reaction wasn't one of exuberant joy at reaching "the best season ever." Rather, I was terrified that this new identity would take the place of the retreat leader, spiritual director, and writer roles that had barely even started. Immediately, I felt convicted about the selfish nature of these thoughts and fears. Of course, I was thrilled by the prospect of a new little life in our family, but the worries persisted. I didn't know who I could talk to about how I was feeling. But then, in His unending grace and perfect timing, God brought me Henri and his little book *Adam*. Through Henri and Fred, God reminded me that—no matter what callings He has given me—loving those around me is my greatest work.

If you ever experience a moment when you don't think you can talk to another soul about the dilemmas you're struggling with, remember that the faithful who have gone before us can help us find our way. As I learned, loving those God had placed in my life didn't mean that the new roles I was excited about had to fall by the wayside. Callings aren't singular. They certainly weren't for Jesus, who loved His mother, disciples, and other friends well even as He did the mighty work of bringing God's kingdom to earth. The same is true for us: We can live into our specific callings even as we offer love in the simplest of ways to the people in our neighborhood.

JOURNAL

- What issue have you been wrestling with that your giant's giants have helped you resolve?

THE GREAT CLOUD OF WITNESSES

Baron Friedrich von Hügel, Evelyn Underhill, and Teresa of Avila all taught me about the gift of the "cloud of witnesses." I learned about the baron by reading books written by Evelyn Underhill. He was the spiritual director of whom she wrote, "I owe [him] my whole spiritual life," and the subject of my doctoral study.

After I immersed myself in his letters, diaries, and academic writing for three years full time, so many ideas began to flood my mind of how the baron had influenced my life. I could hear echoes from his writings constantly. But a few phrases rose to the surface:

- "One thing at a time" has reminded me to be attentive to just one thing rather than being distracted, harried, or overwhelmed by tangents.
- "Wise living requires frequent refusals" has encouraged me not to try to do too much. These words are challenging when there is good work to be done, but they are essential to living well.
- "Moderation in spiritual practices" has emphasized to me the importance of leisurely spirituality and engagement in nonreligious interests.

Overall, his words have encouraged me to enjoy my hobbies of gardening and watching movies, to take sabbath and rest seriously, and to avoid, as the baron would say, the "overworking of body, mind, or soul."

—Robyn Wrigley-Carr, associate professor, University of Divinity,
Australia (Giant: Friedrich von Hügel, philosopher, 1852–1925)

EMBRACING EACH STAGE

Transitions are almost always signs of growth, but they can bring feelings of loss. To get somewhere new, we may have to leave somewhere else behind.

—FRED ROGERS, *Life's Journeys According to Mister Rogers*

As they entered the later stages of their lives, Fred and Henri made similar adjustments to their daily routines and busy schedules. Fred had to cut back on his work on *Mister Rogers' Neighborhood,* eventually ending the show and moving on to other endeavors. Henri, following what his body and spirit were telling him, retired from teaching at the university to live in the L'Arche community. In their own distinct ways, both provided beautiful examples of what it means to age gracefully.

As I've approached my own golden years, I've been surprised at how challenging it is to age gracefully. My body has slowed down. Clothes no longer fit the way they used to. Activities I always enjoyed, like celebrating birthdays or meeting my kids at the park, exhaust me in ways they never did before. No matter how many friends I've observed going through these changes before me, somehow I never thought it would be me—or at least not so soon. This realization has left me wondering if I should fight this new stage of life or embrace it.

In the same way, you might be tempted to cling to the life stage you're in now instead of embracing the next one. Maybe you're about to graduate from the exciting yet safe college years, and the prospect of entering the "real world" to secure a career feels daunting. Or you're about to begin or end a relationship, and you're already missing some of the things you'll have to leave behind. Or you're about to add a baby to the family, and—as happy as you are—you know that your life will never be the same again.

As different as Mister Rogers's and Henri Nouwen's lives were from ours, we can learn a lot from the intentional ways they approached life. They embraced each stage with hearts full of gratitude and focused on the opportunities rather than the losses. They recognized what to prioritize and when to step away. Even as they released things they might have liked to hold on to, they found enjoyment in new experiences.

Perhaps you've noticed similarities between your life stage and a particular season in your giant's life. How might God be speaking to you through those similarities, whether by offering comfort or nudging you to make changes? No matter what stage of life you're in now, may you peacefully receive its joys and even its challenges, knowing that your Father is directing all of them.

JOURNAL

- How is your giant helping you in your current stage of life?

ROUTINE IS UNDERRATED

The *really* important "great" things are never center stage of life's dramas; they're always "in the wings."

—FRED ROGERS, *The World According to Mister Rogers*

red Rogers's alarm clock rang at five every morning. After getting up, he would flip on the light in the living room and sit with a cup of coffee, his Bible, and a notebook. He would read a few passages, think over his day, pray over each part, and then eat breakfast.

Once he left the house, he would head to the health club, where he would swim, shower, and get dressed. Then it was on to the television studio, where he worked the same job for thirty years. When the workday was done, he would go home, eat dinner with his family, make a phone call or write a letter, and then go to bed. He also served on one or two committees and spent the weekends enjoying time with his family and attending church.

Week after week, he held to this routine. Not necessarily the recipe some might expect for a remarkable life. And yet we're still talking about him today. Somehow this one man's mundane life—lived faithfully and consistently—became the subject of books, blogs, podcasts, television shows, and feature-length films. His simple life left a lasting mark.

We live in an age with a skewed sense of what the good life looks like. If you're going to be someone important, you have to hustle hard—wake up early, stay up late, and network like your life depends on it. The twenty-first-century rallying cries of "Go!" "Get!" and "Do!" promise fulfillment and impact.

But the lives of our giants paint a different picture. And so do the lives of countless others who have likely made a powerful impact on you— parents, grandparents, siblings, colleagues, teachers, coaches, and neighbors. Each of them worked, lived, and loved day by day and week by week in their own neighborhoods. Just like Mister Rogers did. Just like you can.

So if you ever catch yourself worrying that your life is too small or insignificant in our fast-paced, adrenaline-saturated, and high-excitement culture, remember that our giants and the everyday heroes in our lives show us there is power and purpose in the routine.

JOURNAL

- How has your giant given you a healthier picture of what a significant life looks like?

PILGRIMAGE PRINCIPLE

DELIGHT IN THE DETOURS

There are two biblical designations for people of faith that are extremely useful: *disciple* and *pilgrim*. *Disciple (mathētēs)* says we are people who spend our lives apprenticed to our master, Jesus Christ. . . . *Pilgrim (parepidēmos)* tells us we are people who spend our lives going someplace, going to God, and whose path for getting there is the way, Jesus Christ.

—EUGENE H. PETERSON, *A Long Obedience in the Same Direction*

You have your pilgrimage planned out to a T: thirty days of walking and five rest days. Everything is going well, and you're already almost halfway to Santiago.

The plan for today was to head to Burgos, fifteen miles away. But as you wandered around town and talked with your hosts from dinner last night, you kept hearing about a monastery two miles off the trail. The Romanesque church, built in the twelfth century and surrounded by a serene landscape, is peaceful and beautiful. Its nativity scene—illuminated by natural light—is apparently like nothing you've ever seen before.

Two miles off the trail doesn't seem like a lot, but that's four extra miles round trip on top of an already-fifteen-mile day, plus spending time at the monastery. Could you do it and still reach Burgos? How much would the detour threaten your schedule?

But you can't shake the sense that a gift is waiting for you in this unexpected detour. So when you reach the marker, instead of continuing straight, you veer to the right, to eager for what God has in store.

• • •

One of the delights of traveling on a giant journey is that you don't know all that will happen. You might encounter divine detours you weren't expecting. Or God might reveal sacred surprises you never could have anticipated.

When you set out on this journey, you mapped your course, thinking you knew the path you would take. But as your journey progresses, you will encounter things you didn't plan on: people who shaped your giant, faith practices from other cultures, places from your giant's life that are beckoning you to visit, or hobbies your giant enjoyed that pique your interest. When you feel the spark of excitement, don't be afraid to follow it. Exploring a side trail is taking an ordained detour that may even prove to be a shortcut to your destination.

These divine detours along the journey with your giant are not disruptions but pieces of God's plan that are just as important as the main trail itself.

JOURNAL

- What divine detours have appeared on your journey that the Spirit may be nudging you to take?

MILE MARKER

The giant journey offers natural moments to pause at the side of the trail. Take time to do this at the end of each month.

FINAL STEPS ON THE TRAIL

- Find a few minutes to slip away to a quiet place. Closing your eyes, breathe in the richness of the moment and ask God to continue His good work in your heart as you review the Pilgrimage Principle and your notes for this month.
- Which one of your giant's giants did you spend your month with? As you think about what this person has taught you, consider why God may have led you to them. Does it seem like your time with them is done, or do you think you should continue with them for another month?
- Halfway through the journey now, take some time to give God thanks, bring Him your questions, and talk to Him about anything that you are troubled or excited about.

REFLECTION

Take some time to reflect on the following questions as you wrap up the month. Your answers can be great indicators of what the Spirit might be leading you to focus on in the month ahead.

Summary: What direction did the Lord take you this month? Did your month go like you thought it would? Were there any unexpected leadings, twists, or turns?

Growth: In what areas of your life do you see growth or shifts in your thinking?

Excitement: When you think about your journey, what fills you with energy?

Challenges: What is bothering you? Do you have any unanswered questions or frustrations related to your journey?

PILGRIM PRAYER

Oh Jesus—the Way, the Truth, and the Life—the adventures of walking with You never cease. Thank You for Your divine detours from my meticulous plans. No matter how much my trail shifts, I know I never need to fear any new turn. I can let go and follow You without knowing the result. Because all You ever want to do is bless me. You've been trying to teach me that for so long. Oh Jesus, guide my heart on Your paths. Amen.

TRAVELOGUE

....

....

....

....

....

....

....

....

....

....

....

....

....

....

....

....

....

....

....

SEASON THREE

PLAY

ENJOY THE JOURNEY

[Thomas] Merton consciously sought out his own guides, most of whom had been dead for hundreds of years. "There are people one meets in books or in life whom one does not merely observe, meet, or know," Merton wrote in *Conjectures of a Guilty Bystander.* "A deep resonance of one's entire being is immediately set up with the entire being of the other. . . . Heart speaks to heart in the wholeness of the language of music; true friendship is a kind of singing."

—Fred Bahnson, "On the Road with Thomas Merton"

STEPS ALONG THE TRAIL

After six months of intense walking with your giant, allow God to continue working in you through a season of play. As you embrace a leisurely stage of the journey, consider these possible focus points for the month ahead:

☐ Pick a resource connected to your giant that can easily travel wherever life takes you (e.g., a book, YouTube series, or podcast), try one of your giant's hobbies for yourself, or enjoy a giant-related excursion (visit a museum or historical site, attend a lecture, etc.).

☐ Take your month's materials and enjoy some of your giant journey study times outdoors.

☐ Remember that God has invited you on a unique journey. Don't worry if none of these focus ideas resonate with you. Just stay attuned to how the Spirit is guiding you.

☐ Complete the weekly journal prompts and the trail guide.

JOURNEY WITH FRED

Check out this resource if you're joining the giant journey with Mister Rogers:

- *The Road to Daybreak: A Spiritual Journey* by Henri Nou-wen

TRAIL GUIDE

Focus: What is your primary focus for this month? How is God directing your journey?

Media: What are you reading, watching, or listening to as you engage with your giant this month?

Quotes: What meaningful quotes would you like to remember from this month?

Experiences: What new places, activities, or events are you experiencing this month because of your giant?

Faith: In what ways has your giant drawn you closer to God this month? What spiritual practices have you engaged in as a result of your giant journey?

Sticky Points: What questions or topics might you want to explore more later?

EMBRACE THE EBB AND FLOW

You saw me before I was born.
  Every day of my life was recorded in your book.
Every moment was laid out
  before a single day had passed.

—Psalm 139:16, NLT

As you step into the second half of the journey, you might be experiencing different emotions. Maybe you feel excited about all you've learned, humbled by the ways God is transforming you, nervous about what may lie ahead, frustrated that you haven't covered more ground, or sad that you're closer to the end than you are to the beginning. Whatever you're bringing with you into the next stage, this season is the perfect time to pause and just enjoy. To slow your walking pace even further and take the opportunity to play.

When I entered month 7 with Fred, my emotions felt like a wildly swinging pendulum. On one hand, I was excited about letting go of structure to see what the month would bring. But on the other, with a spur-of-the-moment trip to Alaska thrown into my schedule, I worried about how God would continue to work in me through the journey, with me flitting all over the planet, unable to truly focus. Not sure what the month might hold, I tossed a copy of Henri Nouwen's book *The Road to Daybreak* into my suitcase and hoped for the best.

As I worked on surrendering my ideas about how the journey was supposed to go, I remembered Fred and Joanne's treasured summer cottage on Nantucket Island off the coast of Massachusetts. They lovingly referred to this hideaway as "The Crooked House" because of how it leaned over with age.

Every summer, they left Pennsylvania and escaped to this house to rest and spend time with family and friends. With eight hundred feet of beachfront on the bay on one side and the ocean on the other, Fred was able to swim every day, leisurely work on scripts, and enjoy fun summer activities. He clearly understood the need to make room for every aspect of life amid the important things he was trying to accomplish. And he did it with a smile.

As I struggled with my convoluted emotions about the Alaska trip, I felt comforted by the reminder of Fred's own yearly summer vacations and his conviction that each person should be encouraged to express all their feelings. One of his bedrock principles was that all feelings are mentionable and manageable, something that he learned from his close friend and adviser on *Mister Rogers' Neighborhood*, psychologist Margaret McFarland.

Emotions were, in fact, so important to Fred that one of the only times he ever stopped taping on *Mister Rogers' Neighborhood* was when an actor mistakenly tried to comfort Daniel Tiger, telling him not to be afraid. Fred stopped right then and there and explained strongly yet graciously that no one—whether puppet or human being—was ever to be told not to feel or express any emotion, positive or negative.

That thought comforted me.

During this month of play, notice how you're feeling. Are you eager and excited for the different pace? Relieved at the opportunity to relax? Or are you afraid that your growth will stop? Are you worried that you might miss something if you take a break from intentional discovery?

Thankfully, God knows our human limitations and is intimately acquainted with our worries and longings. And His work won't stop just because ours does. Our walk with Him is a delicate balance of our efforts melded with His. He knows His plans for us, and His work continues in seasons when we labor diligently and in seasons when—by His design—we play more.

The giant journey, like life, will ebb and flow. In some months, you'll be able to go deeper into study and experiences with your giant, and in others, you'll meander through meadows and laze beside lakes. In both cases, the transformation in you will continue—because this is God's work, not yours.

JOURNAL

- What type of season are you in? How have you embraced months of going deeper and months of taking it easier?

SURPRISED IN THE BEST WAYS

John Calvin surprised me in all the best ways. He modeled how to do your best "to be at peace with all men." Despite differing opinions around him, Calvin weathered the storms of political and religious divides, showing how to love well while holding to his own beliefs. This brought me comfort as our nation walked through tumultuous elections, a pandemic, and racial tensions.

I was most drawn to Calvin's deep love of Scripture. He consistently taught others to prioritize learning Scripture. He put the Bible to song to teach those who were illiterate. He taught children Scripture songs and effortlessly wove Scripture into his conversation.

Lastly, I appreciated seeing Calvin improve his community. He curbed domestic violence by advocating for nightly curfews. With fewer men drinking late into the night, fewer women and children were harmed. His focus went beyond the pulpit to the daily lives of his community.

We would still disagree on double predestination, but oh, would we enjoy a rich conversation about the beauty of Psalms!

—Stacy Holmes, minister, Assemblies of God (Giant: John Calvin, pastor, theologian, Reformer, 1509-64)

GOD'S MISCHIEVOUS WAYS

Discovering the truth about ourselves is a lifetime's work, but it's worth the effort.

—FRED ROGERS, *The World According to Mister Rogers*

A few years ago, with my kids raised, I made a list of what I hoped to do in my new stage of life. At the end of the list, I sheepishly jotted down "Learn to write." I didn't believe it would happen. I had been talking and dreaming about writing my entire adult life and was convinced that everyone I knew was sick of hearing about it, including myself and even God.

But God saw my vulnerable heart. No sooner had I finished my list than I received an email for a week of free training sessions from a Christian writers organization that had never emailed me before. I gleefully jumped in. Since then, I've been learning and honing the craft. I've been especially drawn to memoir.

Then God brought me to Henri Nouwen.

My husband and I joke that God works in mischievous ways, consistently amazing us with surprises that lie beyond the next bend. I can almost imagine God laughing as I reach behind the washing machine for a fallen sock and find a missing ring instead. Or trying to hide a smile as I miss a flight only to have a life-changing conversation with a stranger. Each mysterious occurrence moves us forward on our perfect path. This mischievous side of God appeared when Fred introduced me to Henri.

I could have chosen any one of Henri Nouwen's forty books to read, but the one I was drawn to was *The Road to Daybreak*. As I began reading, I discovered that it not only contained principles that deepened my understanding of God but was also a memoir! As I flipped through the pages, God opened my eyes to the nuances of the genre He had been leading me to.

Fred was well acquainted with God's mischievous ways. He knew that God was not only interested in but also delighted by each person becoming all that He created them to be. As Fred's career path shifted from being a Presbyterian minister to ministering to children through television, God opened the door for him to work at the first public television studio in Pittsburgh with dedicated programming for children, right around the corner from his hometown of Latrobe.

During his time in seminary as he spoke to faculty about his passion to use his degree in children's television, they suggested he intern with psychologist Margaret McFarland, a key figure in child development who *just happened* to be working in Pittsburgh alongside Dr. Benjamin Spock, renowned pediatrician and author of *The Common Sense Book of Baby and Child Care*, and famed psychologist Dr. Erik Erikson. With Fred feeling called to make a difference in child development, he couldn't have been born in a more perfect place than Latrobe, Pennsylvania.

The Lord is always working in our lives in mischievous ways, but I wonder how often we miss the signs. In the same way that we can grow numb to our surroundings when driving the same route to work, we can grow numb to God moving. Even worse, we can forget to ask Him to open doors and then fail to recognize when He opens them anyway. Thankfully, one of the many benefits of the giant journey is that it helps us wake up again to where God is moving and notice the next steps He has for us.

JOURNAL

- How have you seen God working mischievously on your giant journey in an area in which you've longed to grow?

IMPERFECTLY HUMAN

....

One of the strongest things we have to wrestle with . . . is the significance of the longing for perfection in ourselves and in the people bound to us.

—FRED ROGERS, *The World According to Mister Rogers*

D o you ever struggle to live within reasonable limits? Do you ever feel torn into pieces as you try to be the best friend or spouse you can be, accomplish all you can at work, and find some time for fun too?

As I read through Henri's memoir *The Road to Daybreak,* I saw myself. Even though he was deeply devoted to God and known for his love for others, he found living at a healthy pace almost impossible and scolded himself repeatedly for his relentless attachment to work. Even during his sabbatical year, when he was supposed to be resting, he found himself knee deep in a new set of projects. He would often sneak into the office in the wee hours of the night so no one would see him failing to take a break.

Fred struggled with this drive for productivity as well. Overly committed to doing the things he loved, he put off seeing a doctor when his stomach problems became more frequent. By the time he finally made an appointment, his cancer was at an advanced stage, limiting his options for treatment. He died a few months later.

This need to constantly be on the move is a struggle many of us can relate to. My husband and I have always been doing something big on top of our already-full life: building a house, raising a gaggle of children (and, of course, homeschooling), or launching another business or ministry. Whatever it is, we've always pushed to the outer limits of and beyond what we can realistically do well. Our friends have asked us more than once if we will ever settle down.

Henri saw his workaholism and wanted desperately to overcome it. Yet he never did.

I used to think that if we were truly close to Jesus and filled with the same power that raised Him from the dead, we would overcome every weakness. But as I battle my imperfections and observe the holiest people from history struggle till their dying day with their own "thorns in the flesh" (2 Corinthians 12:7–10), I realize that we will never overcome them all. In fact, in a strange way, when I learned that Henri died of a heart attack—possibly the result of his inability to overcome his workaholism—I experienced not only sorrow but also comfort.

Because we're human, we're all going to be a little crazy in our own way. I'm not sure if that's good news or bad. Like the apostle Paul, who was refused when he begged God to remove the thorn he struggled with, none of us living in these human shells will ever overcome every weakness. We won't reach perfection on this side of heaven, and that's okay. Could that be one of the greatest miracles of the gospel—God taking flawed human beings and still doing His work in the world through us?

Fred and Henri are perfect examples of this. Praise God that our giants teach us not only through their strengths how to become more of the glorious people we were created to be but also through their weaknesses how to be at peace with being imperfectly human.

JOURNAL

- How has learning about your giant's weaknesses helped you with yours?

ACROSS CONTINENTS AND GENERATIONS

As I prayed over the list of giants and did some research, I became intrigued by the life of Evelyn Underhill. I noticed similarities in our upbringing and our hunger to know God intimately.

When I found the book *The Ways of the Spirit*—filled with Evelyn's teachings on prayer to church leaders and written in her late fifties and sixties—I knew I wanted to learn from her. At the time, I was the same age, moving into a new season and searching for how to navigate the journey. She had done it well and left her story in vivid color, providing a perfect companion to guide me on my way. Across continents and generations, she could mentor me!

In the richness of her final years, Evelyn wrote, taught, and lived fully into who God created her to be. Her personality and character, as well as her gifts of teaching and prayer, resonated deeply with me. I longed for my gifts to fully ripen and for my life to be used, like hers, for all God intended.

—Sherri Willett, church leader and homemaker
(Giant: Evelyn Underhill, author, lecturer, 1875–1941)

BECOMING A SPIRITUAL GIANT

A life is not important except in the impact it has on other lives.

—JACKIE ROBINSON, *I Never Had It Made*

The "Spiritual Giant League" is not a country club for the rich and famous but a living room open to all those who have faithfully followed God and whose lives are an encouragement to others. Though you may be only at the beginning or middle of your own journey, it's not too early to start thinking and praying about the legacy you will leave behind. As incredible or crazy as it might seem, you might just become a giant in someone else's life someday.

In the same way that a grandparent, historical figure, family friend, or favorite author has had a deep impact on you, you have the potential to leave lasting impressions on the lives of those who come after you— some of whom you may never even meet this side of heaven. How incredible is that?

My father-in-law was a quiet man with a dry sense of humor and unswerving loyalty. He was a hard worker and loved his family and community. Even though he rarely got a word in during our boisterous family gatherings, his life often spoke louder than any voice in the room. I may not be his biological child, but his character deeply formed me. His integrity will forever help me do what is right.

Like my father-in-law and Fred's grandfather, spiritual giants aren't always famous figures. Some are written about in the pages of the Old and New Testaments. Others didn't make it into the Bible but are written about in other books. Still others led lives so quiet and unassuming that they've never been mentioned on a printed page. These faithful followers of Christ who have traveled before us continue to travel with us now through their enduring testaments of faith. Spiritual giants can be as extraordinary as Abraham, Francis of Assisi, or Fred Rogers, or they can be as ordinary as you and me.

Then there are the spiritual giants in training, candidates whose lives are already beginning to show glimmers of the lasting legacies they will leave behind. Some are relatives. Others we go to church with. A handful may walk with us more intimately, caring for us through sickness, the loss of loved ones, struggles with addiction, or the pain of wayward children.

Other giants in training strengthen us from a distance. Authors whose words bring us just what we need on any given day. Podcasters who do their good work through the airwaves. Grocery store workers who stock shelves with food that nourish our bodies.

Each of us can be a spiritual giant in training as we encourage one another on the race of life in big ways and small. Someday, when you have crossed over into heaven, I pray there will be a grand celebration as you enter the band of spiritual giants, and your life continues to strengthen others still on earth.

JOURNAL

- Which everyday mentors in your life are spiritual giants in training? How do you hope to be a spiritual giant for others?

PILGRIMAGE PRINCIPLE

CHALLENGE YOUR COMFORT ZONE

It's one thing to read about being a pilgrim and quite another to actually become one.

—JOYCE RUPP, *Walk in a Relaxed Manner*

After those early days of sleeping in an albergue, the novelty is beginning to wear off. You're starting to miss your bed. You often run out of hot water for your shower, and with twenty other pilgrims sharing the bathroom, you've given up trying to claim a good spot by the sink. And whoever trained Camino hosts in hospitality must have missed the chapter on waiting until at least sunrise to flip on the fluorescent lights. With the rush to get out the door and on the trail by 8:00 A.M., you sometimes feel like you're on a military excursion instead of a pilgrimage! What happened to this being a peaceful, spiritually enriching experience?

Yet despite the constant rush and lack of solitude, the rich moments of the journey continue to surprise you.

Throughout the day, you share deep conversations with other pilgrims along the trail, at meals, or in town. Many of the discussions about faith and life have already proved transformative. In other moments, when you find yourself walking the trail in silence with nothing but your own thoughts, you experience the presence of God differently than you ever have before. The journey is changing you in the best of ways.

Now as you reach the second half of the trail, reflect on what sparked this journey in the first place. You may be aching for your comfy bed, your early-morning quiet time, and your favorite reading chair, but sometimes God calls us to seasons of discomfort. Pilgrims embrace these times of pain knowing there are greater things at work in us through the journey.

• • •

However you might be feeling at the end of month 7, remember that you were created for a purpose. By accepting God's invitation to push beyond your comfort zone, you are making important headway in fulfilling that purpose. So keep moving and take each stretching step. You'll be so glad you did!

JOURNAL

- How is the journey with your giant stretching you beyond your comfort zone and moving you toward your purpose?

MILE MARKER

The giant journey offers natural moments to pause at the side of the trail. Take time to do this at the end of each month.

FINAL STEPS ON THE TRAIL

- During this season of play, let go of intensity and follow the gentler leadings of the Spirit. If you're able, take your materials from this month and do your reflection outdoors as you marvel at the wonder and beauty of God's creation.
- Read through your notes and highlight anything that stands out. Ponder how you have seen God working in the leisurely way you have journeyed with your giant this month. Then spend five minutes with your eyes closed and your hands open as you talk to God and pour out your heart before Him. (It's perfectly okay to set a timer. It can help you feel more relaxed if you're not opening your eyes to check the time.)

REFLECTION

....

Take some time to reflect on the following questions as you wrap up the month. Your answers can be great indicators of what the Spirit might be leading you to focus on in the month ahead.

Summary: What direction did the Lord take you this month? Did your month go like you thought it would? Were there any unexpected leadings, twists, or turns?

Growth: In what areas of your life do you see growth or shifts in your thinking?

Excitement: When you think about your journey, what fills you with energy?

Challenges: What is bothering you? Do you have any unanswered questions or frustrations related to your journey?

PILGRIM PRAYER

Oh Abba Father, You open Your arms wide to little children. You love to dance and sing. You love a good meal, celebrations, and laughter. Help me let go and learn how to play like a child again, even as other demands press in. May a smile spread across my face more often as I drink in a sunset or chat with a friend. Remind me frequently how good You and this life truly are. Amen.

TRAVELOGUE

EMBRACE DISCOMFORT

If I have seen further it is by standing on the shoulders of Giants.

—Isaac Newton, letter to Robert Hooke, 1675

STEPS ALONG THE TRAIL

As you meander along the trail with your giant in this third season, consider these possible focus points for month 8:

☐ Looking at your calendar and what is happening in your life this month, pick a resource or activity that allows you to continue walking with your giant in a way that feels realistic, ready to receive whatever God brings. If you'll be away from home, consider spending an evening at a park, bookstore, or coffee shop. Or if your time this month is limited, keep your chosen resource where you have your morning coffee and read one page per day.

☐ Share your journey with others. If you're going to be traveling, choose a giant-related audiobook to listen to together. Talk about your giant and emulate their godly characteristics.

☐ Remember that God has invited you on a unique journey. Don't worry if none of these ideas resonate with you. Just stay attuned to how the Spirit is guiding you.

☐ Complete the weekly journal prompts and the trail guide.

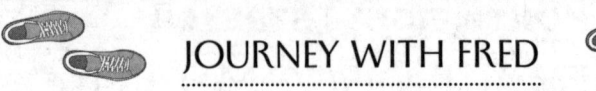

JOURNEY WITH FRED

Check out these resources if you're joining the giant journey with Mister Rogers:

- *Here and Now: Living in the Spirit* by Henri Nouwen
- *The World According to Mister Rogers: Important Things to Remember* by Fred Rogers

TRAIL GUIDE

Focus: What is your primary focus for this month? How is God directing your journey?

Media: What are you reading, watching, or listening to as you engage with your giant this month?

Quotes: What meaningful quotes would you like to remember from this month?

Experiences: What new places, activities, or events are you experiencing this month because of your giant?

Faith: In what ways has your giant drawn you closer to God this month? What spiritual practices have you engaged in as a result of your giant journey?

Sticky Points: What questions or topics might you want to explore more later?

GUIDED DRIFT

Isn't it mysterious how so many wonderful things in life come to us seemingly without our planning? We start traveling down one street, and we find ourselves interested in something we never expected on a side street; and as we explore it, the side street becomes the main road for us.

—FRED ROGERS, *Life's Journeys According to Mister Rogers*

Fred firmly believed in a concept called "guided drift," a foundational principle he learned from his seminary professor Dr. William Orr. It encourages you to view your life as a raft floating down a stream. As your raft floats along, you can put your pole out from time to time to keep from bumping into logs and other obstacles, but the real force propelling your raft along is not the pole but the stream itself. In the same way, our actions and decisions do affect our lives, but God is the one directing the current and moving us forward. So when your life seems like it isn't going the way it should, remembering the guided-drift principle can help take some of the stress and struggle away.

When I entered month 8 with Fred Rogers, my life was starting to sound like a broken record. I returned home from Alaska and hit the ground running. Our first guests soon arrived at the prayer cabin, and I started making preparations for the extended family that would be coming for a two-week reunion.

Even with the happy events filling the month, I missed having more intentional time with my giant. My full schedule meant that I could only squeeze in a few pages from my next Henri Nouwen book, *Here and*

Now, and a quote from *The World According to Mister Rogers* a few times a week. Still, I tried to give myself grace and remember the guided-drift principle.

During some stretches, your journey with your giant might feel less like you're walking side by side on the trail and more like you're staying in two separate albergues and checking in by phone every few days. Either way, God is directing it. Even though you might not be together in the same way, you can still watch for the good things that will arise: a quote from your giant that gives you courage at just the right moment, growth in a giant-related characteristic you've been longing to see develop, or a divine connection related to your journey you weren't expecting. These are just a few ways God will continue to direct your journey, even when you feel like you're barely moving forward.

In the months when your journey is less focused than you would like, do what you can. Imagine yourself and your giant drifting along together on the stream of life as God directs, dangling your feet over the side of the raft, letting your toes float in the cool water, and enjoying the sunshine on your faces.

JOURNAL

- How does the stream of your life look for the month ahead?

- How is the Lord directing you to float along with your giant?

A FELLOW PRISONER

I can relate to Corrie ten Boom because of being in prison myself.

When I'm uncomfortable on my four-inch mattress, I think about Corrie sleeping on a thin layer of straw on the dirt. When I'm frustrated at not being allowed to stand in my doorway and talk, I remember how she wasn't allowed to speak to other inmates at all and would instead talk to the ants.

I remind myself of how God protected Corrie and made her invisible. I often pray that He will make me invisible too. I don't get into drugs or girlfriends, I don't steal or swear, and I'm nice to everyone. I just want to do my time and be done.

Like Corrie, I try to share about Jesus with those I encounter. I feel it's my mission while I'm here. I pray He will take those seeds and make them grow.

God's Word says, "If you forgive other people when they sin against you, your heavenly Father will also forgive you" (Matthew 6:14). I have learned to forgive like Corrie forgave the guards who killed her sister. In the same way He did impossible things in her life, I believe He'll do them in mine, carrying me through every difficulty with His grace until I get to the other side.

—Joy A., inmate (Giant: Corrie ten Boom,
Holocaust survivor, writer, 1892–1983)

WEEK TWO

UNIVERSAL LONGINGS

....

I am always wondering if people who know every part of me, including my deepest, most hidden thoughts and feelings, really do love me.

—HENRI NOUWEN, *The Road to Daybreak*

Henri Nouwen wrestled deeply with loneliness and insecurity. As a Catholic priest, he remained single and so never enjoyed the love and reassurance of a spouse. He had many close friends, colleagues, and students and was renowned all over the world as a teacher, writer, and speaker, yet he still desperately struggled to feel known and loved.

As hard as it might be to believe, Fred grappled with this longing as well. Battling the childhood scars of loneliness, he ached all his life to be assured that he was known and loved. His studio manager, Margy Whitmer, noted this as the reason it was almost impossible for him to get anywhere on time. Fred couldn't help but give every person who stopped him on the street his undivided attention. His affirmation of their worth, driven by a desire to ensure no one ever felt unnoticed or unloved, also fed his insatiable hunger for love and acceptance.

Although I have been married for decades, have six children, and enjoy an enriching career and ministry, I often resonate with Henri's and Fred's sense of insecurity. Even as I spent time with extended family during a happy summer reunion—an event where I should have felt the most known and loved—I felt so alone. But when I remembered how Fred and Henri struggled in similar ways, I realized that these feelings of insecurity affect all of us. Whether you're like Fred Rogers (adored by friends, family, and a worldwide audience), Henri Nouwen (loved by colleagues, friends, and students), or me (surrounded by a wonderful family and a strong community), you will likely still experience moments when you ache with loneliness.

These universal longings link us together as humans and soften our hearts to others who might be struggling with the same things. Some days, you might feel strong, connected, and known. Other days, even when you're surrounded by dozens at the supermarket or hundreds at a church or event venue, you might feel utterly alone. Or perhaps you face other common struggles like fear of death, rejection, physical pain, illness, or grief. Though it may prove to be only a small comfort, your giant likely felt some of these pains of the human experience too. And maybe by observing how your giant handled such challenges, you can be strengthened in overcoming yours as well.

JOURNAL

- What difficult experience of your giant has helped you in your own suffering?

SURPRISED BY FREEDOM

An invasive vine had wrapped itself around the "tree" of my life. Slowly but surely, it was sapping my strength and bringing me down to destruction. That vine was alcoholism. Having lived a devoted Christian life, I was surprised by the relentless nature of this debilitating disease. I was powerless to overcome its grip, just like a tree is helpless beneath a choking vine. I needed someone's help to cut it off.

Along came Bill W.

Bill's help came by way of Alcoholics Anonymous. His story and writing provided a step-by-step program of recovery. There was hope if I admitted I was powerless over alcohol, embraced God's healing power, and surrendered willingly to taking one step at a time, one moment at a time. With the power of God's Holy Spirit, Bill's tools cut away the invasive vine and brought me freedom to be of use to God and my fellows. I thank God for Bill's story and the hope it brought me then and still brings me now.

—Perry Gabbard, program manager, author of *Stepping Out on an Adventure of Faith* (Giant: Bill W. [Wilson], founder of Alcoholics Anonymous, 1895–1971)

WHEN DREAMS MEET REALITY

As we talked, I had the distinct feeling that it will not be easy to be here, but also that I will not be alone in my struggle. I thought, "It is going to be hard but blessed. I am called to this place of weak and broken people. . . . Do not worry, just move into it and trust that you will find what your heart most desires."

—HENRI NOUWEN, *The Road to Daybreak*

When we got home from Alaska, my husband and I raced to get the prayer cabin finished and furnished for guests. Excited to watch the vision God had given us years before unfold, we welcomed our first two retreaters. Unfortunately, both experiences resulted in less-than-ideal outcomes, and my joy was shattered by tears. I became frustrated and discouraged. During my quiet time, I could barely focus. I journaled a little. Then I opened my Bible. It helped, yet my soul still felt ragged.

Finally, I turned to my "cloud of witnesses" for strength. As I opened my Henri Nouwen book, I prayed that God would speak. To my surprise, the Spirit began ministering to me the moment I read the next chapter title: "A Hard but Blessed Vocation."

Exactly! Here again was God, working in mischievous ways.

In that chapter, Henri wrote about his first day in his new position at the L'Arche Daybreak community for the disabled. After experiencing the richness of the community during his sabbatical year, he was excited for his new role. But that excitement quickly gave way to the feeling that he was in way over his head, as it often does when dreams meet reality.

Fred wasn't immune to feeling overwhelmed either. After eleven years of great success with *Mister Rogers' Neighborhood*, when all people saw on the outside was one great program after another, he sat in anguish behind closed doors and wrestled to write the next episode. In a note to himself in 1979, he wrote,

> Am I kidding myself that I'm able to write a script again? . . . Why can't I trust myself? . . . AFTER ALL THESE YEARS, IT'S JUST AS BAD AS EVER. I wonder if every creative artist goes through the tortures of the damned trying to create? GET TO IT, FRED! . . . But don't let anybody ever tell anybody else that it was easy. It wasn't.*

There's no way to know how much obedience will cost you before you live it. Somewhere along the way, you will likely realize how powerless you are in your own strength to complete whatever task you are called to. But the fulfillment you will experience when you persevere will truly be unmatched.

So when your pie-in-the-sky ideals are countered with a heavy dose of reality, remember how Henri felt in way over his head on his first day, how Fred wrestled with every script, or how your giant battled to do what God called them to do. Remember and turn your eyes to God. He will be there to help, just like He was for them.

JOURNAL

- How has your giant helped you embrace the hardship of your calling?

---

* Maxwell King, *The Good Neighbor: The Life and Work of Fred Rogers* (Abrams, 2018), 315–16.

BETWEEN WORLDS

Anyone who intends to come with me has to let me lead. You're not in the driver's seat; *I* am. Don't run from suffering; embrace it. Follow me and I'll show you how.

—Matthew 16:24, MSG

Fred Rogers was raised Presbyterian and became an ordained minister. In the summers, he attended the Anglican church on Nantucket Island. He also attended mass at Saint Vincent Archabbey and received Catholic last rites at his bedside just days before he died. He was a person with his feet in multiple spheres of the Christian faith.

When I took a closer look at the threads of my life, I realized I was too. I was raised Episcopalian, attended Catholic school, met the Lord through an Assemblies of God youth group, and have spent my adult years in nondenominational Bible churches. I discovered spiritual direction and the giant journey at a Catholic training center, and I now run a retreat facility that welcomes a wide range of believers in the Christian faith.

One summer, when planning my own spiritual retreat, I stumbled upon an advertisement for one led by Father Timothy Gallagher, a renowned Catholic priest and author I greatly admired. In holy oblivion, I jumped in.

When I arrived, I immediately found myself surrounded by little circles of priests, nuns, and other Catholic believers jabbering excitedly about "Father so-and-so" and this diocese or that one. Everything in me screamed that I had made a big mistake. But even with my wild emotions, I felt God confirming that *He* had called me there and was inviting me to trust Him.

Later, as I chatted with a friendly attendee, she shared her excitement about being on this retreat with Father Gallagher.

"Not to mention Father Boniface Hicks," she said. "Can you believe he is here to serve as chaplain?"

"Who is Father Boniface?" I asked.

She had barely finished her explanation when Father Boniface himself soon entered the small living room. Interrupting herself, she urged him to tell the story of his conversion, along with some of her other favorite stories from his YouTube channel.

As we transitioned into our small groups, I ended up being assigned to Father Boniface's group. It was then that I found out he *just happened* to be from Latrobe, Pennsylvania, and was a professor at Saint Vincent Archabbey. There, right in front of me, was a connection to Fred's hometown, the Fred Rogers Institute, and Fred's experience with the Catholic faith!

As thankful as I am for my exposure to many expressions of faith in the Christian tradition, it's not easy to live in multiple denominational worlds. They don't always understand one another, and at times, uncomfortable divisions exist. Sometimes I feel that life would be simpler if I were in only one. But I also know that my life has been inarguably enriched by my experiences in different denominations. After all, God's work isn't affected by the boundary lines we humans have drawn between ourselves.

We should be careful not to limit God's work in our lives. Maybe for you the limit isn't a denominational boundary but one of timing or circumstance. Often, we aren't even aware of these boundaries until we experience the discomfort of God gently pulling them away.

In those moments, we may sense a tug-of-war in our souls, stirred by a question from the Spirit that all believers must face along their life's journey: "Are you willing?"

Answering that question isn't always easy, but consider what you could miss out on if you say no. Saying yes may feel uncomfortable but at the same time offer you gifts that you haven't received before.

JOURNAL

- During your giant journey, what unfamiliar spheres have you sensed God nudging you to explore that you might have been unwilling to enter before?

PILGRIMAGE PRINCIPLE

ANTICIPATE OBSTACLES

Pilgrimages rarely go as planned. They're evolving journeys, not packaged holidays.

—TED HARRO, "A Journey in Humility," *Renovaré* podcast

Two-thirds of the way to Santiago, you've overcome the mighty Pyrenees mountains, the rain, stifling heat, blisters, and tendonitis. You're almost home free! After battling another mountainous stretch yesterday, you're enjoying a gloriously flat walk through green pastures. You've heard about the beautiful sunflower fields and melodious bells of grazing cows that you will encounter on this stage of the journey.

But no one said anything about the Montes de León—one of the steepest climbs of the entire trail. You thought you were done with mountains, yet there they are.

Exhausted and frustrated, you rant to God, "I've done enough! I can't take any more!" But when you finish your tirade, the mountains are still standing there in front of you.

Just as often happens in life, your relaxing journey has been interrupted in a split second by a challenge you weren't expecting.

• • •

Justin Skeesuck and Patrick Gray met when they were five years old and became lifelong friends. Connected by their faith and Idaho roots, they faced life's joys and challenges together, especially when Justin's neuromuscular disease began to decrease his mobility dramatically. In 2014, these two courageous friends set out on the Camino, Justin in his wheelchair and Patrick—along with a few other friends—planning to push him the entire way.

Near the end of their trek and after a ten-and-a-half-hour ascent up the mountains, they paused to rest in the grass. Relaxing their sore muscles, they gazed up at the blue sky and back at the town they had left that morning. As they prepared to move on, they turned toward the trail ahead and were filled with dismay. The path was covered with shattered boulders and earth "as if a staircase collapsed." There was absolutely no way they could navigate such terrain with Justin's chair. But they had come prepared for just such an occasion. Patrick and a friend pulled out a body sling, slid the fabric underneath Justin, and began trudging up the trail. Even though their progress was slow, they were able to keep going and finish the trail together.*

Just like when traveling the Camino, we never know what the journey with our giant will bring. Some people will experience long, challenging stretches with a lot of inner healing. These parts of the journey can feel like agonizing mountainous terrain. For others, the work may be less strenuous, making the trail feel gloriously flat and scenic.

No matter what your journey looks like today, remember that God is directing every step. If you're facing a rocky stretch when you were hoping for a break, take a deep breath and trust that your faithful Guide has provided everything you need. Then take your next step. The rewards will be so worth it!

JOURNAL

- How has your giant journey been different than you expected?

- Has it felt more mountainous or gloriously flat and scenic?

---

* Patrick Gray and Justin Skeesuck, *I'll Push You: A Journey of 500 Miles, Two Best Friends, and One Wheelchair* (Tyndale Momentum, 2017), 71–72.

MILE MARKER

The giant journey offers natural moments to pause at the side of the trail. Take time to do this at the end of each month.

FINAL STEPS ON THE TRAIL

- Settle into one of your favorite quiet spaces. Prayerfully read through your notes, highlight the things that stand out to you, and fill in any prompts you haven't yet.
- Remove all distractions and sit back with your feet on the floor. Sit quietly for five to ten minutes. Close your eyes and ask the Spirit to show you how your giant's characteristics, worldview, spiritual life, or manner of living has shaped you in the way God intended over the last eight months. Be still. Notice what you hear the Spirit say, what images come to your mind, or what desires rise in your heart.

REFLECTION

Take some time to reflect on the following questions as you wrap up the month. Your answers can be great indicators of what the Spirit might be leading you to focus on in the month ahead.

Summary: What direction did the Lord take you this month? Did your month go like you thought it would? Were there any unexpected leadings, twists, or turns?

Growth: In what areas of your life do you see growth or shifts in your thinking?

Excitement: When you think about your journey, what fills you with energy?

Challenges: What is bothering you? Do you have any unanswered questions or frustrations related to your journey?

PILGRIM PRAYER

Almighty God, more powerful than the waves of the ocean or the thunder that claps in the sky, You have made me in Your image. That means I am powerful, too, even when I don't feel like it. When challenges come, stir up the strength You have planted within me. When what You're asking of me seems too hard, remind me to reach out for Your hand. You'll be there, helping me become more than I ever thought I could be—all for Your kingdom and Your glory. Amen.

TRAVELOGUE

ACCEPT THE INVITATION

We don't yet see things clearly. We're squinting in a fog, peering through a mist. But it won't be long before the weather clears and the sun shines bright! We'll see it all then, see it all as clearly as God sees us, knowing him directly just as he knows us!

But for right now, until that completeness, we have three things to do to lead us toward that consummation: Trust steadily in God, hope unswervingly, love extravagantly.

—1 Corinthians 13:12–13, MSG

STEPS ALONG THE TRAIL

After a couple of lighter months on the trail, you should be feeling a renewed sense of energy. As you progress on your journey, consider these focus points for month 9:

☐ Look back over the last couple of months and think about whether there is anything you feel you aren't finished exploring yet and want to continue digging into.

☐ Flip back to the beginning of the book and review the reasons you chose your giant, the three things you were most interested in learning, and your prayer. Make a list of what you still want to delve into before the journey is done.

☐ Remember that God has invited you on a unique journey. Don't worry if these ideas don't resonate with you. Just stay attuned to how the Spirit is guiding you.

☐ Complete the weekly journal prompts and the trail guide.

JOURNEY WITH FRED

Check out these resources if you're joining the giant journey with
Mister Rogers:

- *Kindness and Wonder: Why Mister Rogers Matters Now More
  Than Ever* by Gavin Edwards
- *Life's Journeys According to Mister Rogers: Things to Remember
  ber Along the Way* by Fred Rogers

TRAIL GUIDE

Focus: What is your primary focus for this month? How is God
directing your journey?

Media: What are you reading, watching, or listening to as you engage with your giant this month?

Quotes: What meaningful quotes would you like to remember
from this month?

Experiences: What new places, activities, or events are you experiencing this month because of your giant?

Faith: In what ways has your giant drawn you closer to God this month? What spiritual practices have you engaged in as a result of your giant journey?

Sticky Points: What questions or topics might you want to explore more later?

WHEN DIFFERENT PATHS EMERGE

....

> Walking could turn out to be the most significant spiritual act in which
> we will ever engage.
>
> —Eugene H. Peterson, foreword to *The Way Is*
> *Made by Walking* by Arthur Paul Boers

When Fred graduated from seminary with a passion and divine call to work in children's television, he was disappointed to find that all the doors seemed to be closing. He had everything he needed to do his most important work—except a television program. And there were none in sight. He didn't even have a temporary job in the meantime, since he'd left his position on *The Children's Corner* on WQED during his final year of seminary to focus on his studies. And even though he was ordained as a Presbyterian minister, the church refused to give any of their resources to television. He had to wonder if his television dream was over before it even began.

As I drove home from the spiritual retreat led by Father Gallagher, I felt some of the same uncertainty about the future that Fred must have felt. I sensed I was done taking my side trail with Henri Nouwen and wondered if I should circle back to focusing solely on Fred. Then my thoughts floated back to the weekend I'd just experienced and the hip, mysterious Father Boniface. Could he be another side trail God was inviting me to explore?

Suddenly feeling joy, excitement, and energy, I marveled at how God had orchestrated my meeting this completely out-of-the-box priest who shared Fred's hometown. I was sure that God was pointing me to Father

Boniface's books, podcast, and healing retreats, and I began to dive into them as soon as I returned home.

To my surprise and disappointment, my exploration didn't take me further on my journey with Fred. Father Boniface's work and ministry were powerful. Yet, none of them led to the divine spark I'd expected as I followed what I'd thought was a powerful leading of the Spirit. I soon found myself floundering a bit on my journey.

As we do our best to follow the leading of the Spirit, our journey doesn't always lead to the places we think it will. When things go differently than we think they should, our temptation might be to clench our fists and try to make something happen. But our greatest fulfillment will never come through our efforts alone. Sometimes what looks like a dead end is the most direct route to everything we are seeking.

Thankfully, even when doors close or expectations aren't met, we can trust that the Lord is still leading our journey. Just as Fred experienced as he sought to follow his call to work in television, we, too, might feel like the answers are delayed or the destination is out of reach. But in the end, none of God's plans will fall short.

JOURNAL

- When have you sensed yourself trying to control the journey with your giant instead of trusting the Lord to lead you?

- Can you recall a time when you followed what you believed was a leading from the Spirit, only for it to turn out differently than you had hoped?

EXPAND YOUR FAITH

In loving and appreciating our neighbor, we're participating in something truly sacred.

—FRED ROGERS, commencement address
at Marquette University, May 2001

One of the greatest gifts Fred gave the world was being a person of faith who appreciated people from many different cultures, ethnicities, intellectual perspectives, and spiritual backgrounds. With a profound respect for people such as Mahatma Gandhi, who were significantly different from himself, Fred taught his listeners not to be threatened by differences but instead to approach them as opportunities to learn more about what makes each of us unique.

As someone who was comfortable in a very specific and traditional faith environment, I was wary of practices that I deemed "other." In truth, I was judgmental and afraid of most expressions of faith that weren't part of my experience.

This nervousness came strongly into play as I held a little laminated card I'd received during the spiritual retreat led by Father Gallagher. The card featured a picture of Saint Ignatius on one side and two of his famous prayers on the other. Although the prayers gripped me and expressed the same sentiments that were in my heart, I worried that even owning a card like this went against my faith tradition. As I explained in the introduction, I didn't want to elevate a saint above God. Would praying the words of a saint lead me onto shaky ground? Would it unnecessarily complicate my faith journey and my unity with the others of my denomination?

As I prayed for wisdom, I sensed God revealing an area where I'd been closed off and guilty of elevating my comfort over His power. Of believing that my specific faith circle was the only God-ordained one in all of Christendom. Who was I to tell God that He couldn't use the prayers of a revered church father from a different faith tradition to speak directly to my heart?

Isn't that one of the most glorious things about walking with a giant? They help us step out of our little cul-de-sac of faith into the wider world of God's kingdom by opening the door to the teachings and perspectives of God's people throughout the centuries. They remind us of the longevity and magnitude of a shared faith that has endured across generations and empires.

One of the many assurances I gained from Fred is that we can show reverence for and childlike curiosity about all faith traditions while maintaining and growing in our own. Listening to and befriending those who were different from him didn't change his beliefs. Instead, it allowed him to love as Jesus loved. And in some ways, it even expanded his faith.

So, though it might be uncomfortable or scary at times, open yourself to how God might be leading you to explore different expressions of the Christian faith. After all, He's not limited by the bounds of any one denomination or tradition. And neither are we.

JOURNAL

- What new expressions of faith has the Lord brought into your life through the walk with your giant?

INSPIRED BY A MAJOR LEAGUE PLAYER

Jackie Robinson's faith in God empowered him to smash the color barrier in major league baseball and to powerfully promote civil rights after his playing days ended.

As a Christian historian, I experienced a deepening of my own faith as I researched and reflected on Robinson's life. I wrote *Strength for the Fight: The Life and Faith of Jackie Robinson* (2022) in large part to explain how the baseball star's strong trust in God equipped him to combat substantial racial prejudice, extensive verbal and physical abuse, numerous threats to his life, and staunch opposition as he strove to improve the circumstances of people of color.

His life provides a model for Christians as we work to upgrade material conditions and promote social justice in contemporary society.

Like us, Robinson was inspired by other believers, most notably his mother, Mallie; his pastor in Pasadena, Karl Downs; and Brooklyn Dodgers general manager, Branch Rickey.

I preached a sermon at the church I serve in Wilmington, North Carolina, on how Downs influenced Robinson's faith formation to help parishioners realize how God can use them to encourage others in their walk with Christ.

—Gary Smith, professor emeritus at Grove City College, author
of *Strength for the Fight: The Life and Faith of Jackie Robinson*
(Giant: Jackie Robinson, professional baseball player, 1919–72)

TRUST THE FATHER

Though Rogers was an ordained Presbyterian minister devoted to the teachings of Jesus of Nazareth, he was equally a spiritualist, in the sense that he had a broad, inclusive view of the human spirit and how to reach it.

—MAXWELL KING, *The Good Neighbor*

Even though his personal Christian faith was solid and steadfast, Fred Rogers maintained a healthy curiosity about other beliefs and religions throughout his life. Beside his bed was a bookshelf including texts such as *Zen Lessons, The Way of Chuang Tʒu, The Ragamuffin Gospel, A Grammatical Analysis of the Greek New Testament,* and *The Sayings of the Buddha.* Though he didn't hold any of these books at the same level as the Bible, he understood the importance of cultivating an awareness of the world and the different perspectives within it.

If your giant journey has introduced you to faith traditions or practices that are different from what you're used to, know that you're not alone. Having been introduced to the rich and sensory aspects of a different denomination's communion practice during my recent spiritual retreat, I found myself missing many of those when practicing communion at my church. Kneeling on the bench in humility and adoration. Speaking words of repentance as I remembered what Christ did for me. Witnessing the reverence of the priest as he lifted the bread and wine toward heaven.

I felt stirred but also conflicted. As grateful as I was for the opportunity to experience the unique gifts of another denomination, I was also afraid of what it might mean for my future in the faith community I'd loved for so long. Was this a threat to my contentment in my own denomination? Did this longing I felt mean that I belonged somewhere else?

When I explained my fears to my spiritual director, she showed me a picture of a suspension bridge she and her husband had walked across. She told me that seeing the bridge was exhilarating and then terrifying. It would take courage to cross. Going first, her husband held her gaze and said, "Just hang on to me and keep looking straight ahead. Once you get your footing, you might even enjoy it."

In explaining the metaphor, my spiritual director said that our trails of faith can often be exhilarating but they can also feel like crossing that narrow suspension bridge. When we come to those newer or uncertain sections of our journey, we can rest assured that the Lord is looking back at us, His hand extended, and saying, "Come on. Hold on to Me. Keep your eyes looking straight ahead. You're going to love this!"

Imagine feeling safe enough to regularly receive from other theological, scientific, and cultural perspectives without fear, knowing that the God of the universe is holding you securely and has been moving in billions of people for thousands of years. Our foundation in Christ is strong. We don't need to close our eyes or run the other way; instead, we can receive the nourishing gifts God has for us.

Stepping out of your comfort zone of faith won't be easy. Most of us like sameness and predictable environments where we don't have to try new things, but God often calls us to something different and even better. When we accept His invitation and step out in faith, we find connection with brothers and sisters we may never have noticed before.

Appreciating other faith practices doesn't mean you have to change your denomination or label one faith community "good" and another "bad." God might just be inviting you to notice. Or He might be calling you to experience a different side of Him by worshipping in a new way. So thank Him for His stirrings in your life. Your experience of other expressions of the Christian faith is giving you an increased love for Him and His people.

JOURNAL

- How has your perspective of your denomination changed since you started walking with your giant?

OPEN YET SECURE

....

The remarkable thing about fearing God is that when you fear God you fear nothing else, whereas if you do not fear God you fear everything else.

—OSWALD CHAMBERS, *The Pilgrim's Song Book*

Fred loved Native American people. In one episode of *Mister Rogers' Neighborhood*, he came in the front door carrying a suitcase. Inside the suitcase was a colorful Native American jacket, moccasins, and a beaded necklace. After telling viewers to close their eyes for a surprise, he then pulled out a magnificent headdress. Though he likely wouldn't do this now because of changing concerns about appropriation, he wore each of the pieces for the rest of the episode. Of course, his heart in doing this was to offer respect and attention to Indigenous American people and their rich cultures, as evidenced by the fact that he featured two videos showing traditional dances and by the way that he explained to children how we could learn from the beauty and closeness of Native American families.

To celebrate our anniversary this month, my husband and I flew to South Dakota to experience the annual Buffalo Roundup at Custer State Park. On our first day there, we headed to the Crazy Horse Memorial and arrived just in time to watch a twenty-seven-year-old Native American woman perform a hoop dance. She told us her name, Brave Flower, had been given to her by her grandfather at her coming of age. He had seen deep within her a woman of strength emerging from a timid young girl who had struggled with many fears. One of the greatest of these fears was public speaking. Yet there she was in front of the crowd, powerfully bridging the gap between cultures and boldly preserving her heritage.

As I listened to her story, tears filled my eyes. I saw myself in her. I was also a woman with many fears that I didn't want to prevent me from completing the important tasks I was created to accomplish. I was fighting a battle she had already won. But seeing her victory over her own fears encouraged me in my journey. Her story had a profound impact on mine.

Imagine what would have happened if I'd allowed the differences between our cultures to form a barrier between us. If I'd put up a wall of prejudice, I might never have received the gift of her life story and how it spoke to mine.

Too often we have the tendency to close ourselves off to other cultures—afraid that if we open the door to anything "other," we might be led astray in our beliefs.

While our faith is never something we should treat flippantly, we should also be slow to judge and slow to fear how others express their beliefs. I don't remember Fred ever being afraid of that. He spoke often about the treasure found in each person and was always fascinated by other cultures. Yet despite his openness to appreciating other people's stories, he remained strong in his own faith and never strayed from his devotion to Christ.

Wouldn't it be fantastic to live like that? Open to experiencing different cultures and receiving the gifts they might offer you, secure in the belief that God is holding you in your devotion to Him? That level of faith is one we should all strive to cultivate.

JOURNAL

- How has the journey with your giant helped you receive from other cultures?

GOD OF ALL NATIONS

Growing up as a missionary kid among Indigenous American communities in western Canada, I was surrounded by Native spirituality from birth. My parents planted a church with a tribal group in British Columbia. As a young adult, I was part of that and have stayed in touch with the Native thought leaders, theologians, and spiritual leaders.

My interest is very personal, as Native spirituality has shaped my worldview from my earliest days. I also did my thesis research on Jonathan Edwards, a renowned theologian and missionary to a Native tribe.

Recently, I was drawn to walk with Black Elk because of my connection to Native people. I was intrigued by the spirituality he discovered in childhood and the divine visions he experienced before converting to Christianity. I hope to continue to grow in faith, welcome experiences beyond my understanding, and celebrate the God who reveals Himself in every culture—not as a threat to Christology but as evidence of Him drawing all people to Himself.

—Nathan Smith, Medicare agent, Bible teacher, spiritual director
(Giant: Black Elk, medicine man, Oglala Lakota people, 1863–1950)

PILGRIMAGE PRINCIPLE

EMBRACE THE KINGDOM

> You are Christ's body—that's who you are! You must never forget this. Only as you accept your part of that body does your "part" mean anything.
>
> —1 Corinthians 12:27, MSG

At mile 4 of your seventeen-mile day, you stop at a roadside stand for coffee and fresh-squeezed orange juice. Glancing at the line forming behind you, you see pilgrims of diverse ethnicities and ages. The multilingual buzz of conversation fills the air in a way that is vastly different from what you would hear in a coffee shop at home.

You think about the faces of all those you've met over the last few weeks on the trail. You've enjoyed countless life-shaping conversations with people with whom you never would have crossed paths in your ordinary life. Even when you haven't shared the same language, you've been able to communicate using gestures, smiles, and laughter. Somehow being on the same trail has given you a deep connection that make words unnecessary.

As you wait to order, joy envelops you. You experience a new fulfillment in your soul from your bond with these beautiful pilgrims sharing the Camino with you. And in that moment, you realize you never want to be without this connection again.

• • •

When we journey with a giant, we can be freed from our individualist mindsets by choosing intentional community with other believers throughout history. The shared experience and expanded worldview ignite in us a desire to learn and receive from others. By sharing the journey with them, we realize we were made not for sameness but for community in all its forms.

In 1 Corinthians 12, Paul explained that God's people are like a body—one part a hand, another a foot, another an eye, and so on. But many of us stop at the words and don't bother with actual application to our own lives. "Oh yes," we agree. "Absolutely. Isn't that beautiful!" And then we walk away and try to live by ourselves, cut off from others. We think we have everything we need—being a hand or a foot or an eye—and believe we can be independent from anyone who might be just a little too different from us. But imagine how horrifying and useless a hand or a foot would be if unattached to the rest of a body!

As you know from traveling nine months with your giant, the mysterious wonder of the body of Christ is that it includes not only those alive with us now but also those who have gone before us. These members of the body are just as vital for our healthy life with God as those we might see every day. Each one offers special gifts that have the power to transform us.

A pilgrimage or the giant journey opens our eyes to how crippled we are without all our other parts. And once we experience the body in all its fullness, we'll never want to go back to trying to live on our own again.

JOURNAL

- How have you viewed your need for the complete and diversified body of Christ before now?

- How do you view it now that you've been journeying with your giant?

MILE MARKER

The giant journey offers natural moments to pause at the side of the trail. Take time to do this at the end of each month.

FINAL STEPS ON THE TRAIL

- Find a quiet place and maybe light a candle. As you sit or kneel, with your eyes open or closed, take a deep breath, and begin your time with five minutes in silent prayer. Whenever your mind wanders, simply say the name of God that is closest to your heart today—Father, Jesus, or Holy Spirit.
- Slowly read through your notes, filling in any prompts you might have missed. When you're done, sit back or kneel again and bring God your praise, questions, and fears. Or you can sit with your hands open in silence and just listen for His voice.
- Jot down anything you sense God saying to you.

REFLECTION

Take some time to reflect on the following questions as you wrap up the month. Your answers can be great indicators of what the Spirit might be leading you to focus on in the month ahead.

Summary: What direction did the Lord take you this month? Did your month go like you thought it would? Were there any unexpected leadings, twists, or turns?

Growth: In what areas of your life do you see growth or shifts in your thinking?

Excitement: When you think about your journey, what fills you with energy?

Challenges: What is bothering you? Do you have any unanswered questions or frustrations related to your journey?

PILGRIM PRAYER

Oh Lord, Faithful One, thank You for Your work in my life. Thank You for challenging me, taking me into new places, and introducing me to others in Your kingdom from different ethnicities, cultures, religious expressions, and times. Thank You for working throughout time in Your people. Thank You for guiding me out of my cul-de-sac of faith into other glorious neighborhoods of Your world. My life is richer because of it. I can't wait to spend eternity exploring all of them. Faithful One, use this experience to deepen my relationship with You. Amen.

TRAVELOGUE

SEASON FOUR

TRANSFORM

SACRED SERENDIPITY

All pilgrimage—whether one day, one month or an entire lifetime—
unfolds before [us] as God leads and we are invited to follow.

—ARTHUR PAUL BOERS, *The Way Is Made by Walking*

STEPS ALONG THE TRAIL

As your journey continues to grow richer in the first month of the
final season, consider these possible focus points:

☐ Choose a topic from the list you made in month 9 or look
back at your notes from the start of the journey and think
about what you want to explore in the time you have left.

☐ Ponder what has stood out to you from your giant's life
and pay attention to any ways God might be calling you to
be more active in your neighborhood, community, or faith
organizations.

☐ Remember that God has invited you on a unique journey.
Don't worry if these ideas don't resonate with you. Just
stay attuned to how the Spirit is guiding you.

☐ Complete the weekly journal prompts and the trail guide.

 ## JOURNEY WITH FRED

Check out these resources if you're joining the giant journey with
Mister Rogers:

• *The World According to Mister Rogers: Important Things to
Remember* by Fred Rogers

- *Deep and Simple: A Spiritual Path for Modern Times* by Bo Lozoff
- *Listening Below the Noise: The Transformative Power of Silence* by Anne D. LeClaire
- Mister Rogers's song lyrics

TRAIL GUIDE

Focus: What is your primary focus for this month? How is God directing your journey?

Media: What are you reading, watching, or listening to as you engage with your giant this month?

Quotes: What meaningful quotes would you like to remember from this month?

Experiences: What new places, activities, or events are you experiencing this month because of your giant?

Faith: In what ways has your giant drawn you closer to God this month? What spiritual practices have you engaged in as a result of your giant journey?

Sticky Points: What questions or topics might you want to explore more later?

PERFECT WORDS

···

The older I get, the more convinced I am that the space between communicating human beings can be hallowed ground.

—FRED ROGERS, *You Are Special*

B o Lozoff was an author, spiritual teacher, and activist who often spoke the perfect words at the right moment in Fred Rogers's life. His book *Deep and Simple* guided Fred in navigating important events, decisions, and challenges. In fact, Fred found the book to be so transformative that he ordered numerous copies at a time and gifted them to people throughout his career. The title itself became a central part of Fred's personal philosophy and work in children's media.

Fred's own words proved to be powerful lifelines at just the right moment to people who needed them. One such person was actress Lauren Tewes, known for her role as the cruise director on *The Love Boat,* an ABC series that ran from 1977 to 1986. Her life had been spiraling out of control because of a cocaine addiction when she heard from a television set in another room, "It's a beautiful day in this neighborhood. Won't you be my neighbor?" In that moment, God spoke to her through those perfect words, and Lauren knew she wasn't alone. Fred's simple words gave her enough hope to begin moving toward a cocaine-free life.*

As I read through one of Fred's books of quotes and looked up the lyrics of his most popular *Neighborhood* songs during my tenth month of

---

* Gavin Edwards, *Kindness and Wonder: Why Mister Rogers Matters More Now Than Ever* (Dey Street, 2019), 148.

journeying with him, his words filled me with courage and inspiration. On one morning in particular—when I was already feeling the pressure of the day's full schedule of housework, appointments, and preparations for the upcoming retreat—I came upon this quote in *The World According to Mister Rogers:*

> I hope you're proud of yourself for the times you've said "yes," when all it meant was extra work for you and was seemingly helpful only to somebody else.*

Struck by how apt those words were for what I was called to do that day, I closed my eyes and let the quote water my thirsty soul. I was then reminded (no doubt by the Holy Spirit) of a statement from my previous giant, Francis of Assisi: "I have done what was mine to do; may Christ teach you what you are to do."† As both quotes settled over me, calming my spinning mind, my heart whispered, "Yes. Even with the struggle, that is what life is all about."

No matter how busy your days might be, may you never take for granted the gift of serving your friends and family, the responsibility of leading your team well, or the privilege of being a part of God's wonderful work. Instead, as your giant's words strengthen you at just the right time, may you be empowered to change the world by doing what is yours to do.

JOURNAL

- What perfect words have you received from your giant at just the right time?

---

* Fred Rogers, *The World According to Mister Rogers: Important Things to Remember* (Hyperion, 2003), 113.

† Thomas of Celano, *St. Francis of Assisi: First and Second Life of St. Francis with Selections from The Treatise on the Miracles of Blessed Francis,* trans. and ed. Placid Hermann (Franciscan Herald, 1988), 309.

A KINDRED SPIRIT

Madeleine L'Engle was brought to my attention by a trusted artist friend. It was as if God were waiting for me to accept the invitation to meet her, as He kept bringing her across my path. One day, I decided to run into a secondhand shop on a whim. As I walked up to a shelf of books, my eyes immediately landed on Madeleine's four-book series, *The Crosswicks Journals.* I was astounded.

Later, when snuggling into bed and opening the first book to check it out, I noticed a scribbled inscription on a piece of paper in the middle of the book. It directed me to the front of the book, where Madeleine herself had signed the copy that I was holding. I knew then that God had plans for this connection with this woman.

I had been feeling a need for wisdom and direction in my art. I had been feeling a bit lost after my mother's prolonged mental illness and passing, and I was very open to having a seasoned woman who had gone before me show me her journey. I had prayed for a mentor who would celebrate my quirkiness, understand my struggles as an artist, and help me give that part of myself fully to God. I found that woman in Madeleine!

—Julie Blakely, administrative assistant

(Giant: Madeleine L'Engle, writer, 1918–2007)

MORE THAN JUST A GIFT

Every gift which is given, even though it be small, is, in reality, great, if it is given with affection.

—PINDAR

In the late 1930s and early 1940s, television became available for people to have in their homes. In 1952, 242 channels were designated for educational television. WQED in Pittsburgh was the fifth of these channels and the first to be community sponsored. As the station prepared to go on the air for the first time with very little cash and no programs of its own, station manager Dorothy Daniel hired two energetic young professionals—Josie Carey and Fred Rogers—with the goal of developing an exceptional program for children.

Like Fred, Josie was from the Pittsburgh area. As a member of a boisterous Italian family, she was charismatic and a natural storyteller. Enthralled with listening to the radio growing up, she had developed a passion for educating and entertaining children.

Fred and Josie hit it off and immediately started brainstorming ideas for children's programs. Though they had been hired to host separate programs, they soon had a concept for a collaborative program instead. They pitched their idea to Dorothy, who immediately saw the genius in their partnership and gave them an enthusiastic "Yes!"

On the night before the station went live, Dorothy hosted a dinner for all the staff and included with each place setting a gift to show her appreciation for each person's hard work. When Fred opened his gift, he found a small orange tiger puppet. Even though Dorothy hadn't seen Fred acting with his puppets yet, she knew he had an interest in puppetry and had bought the gift on impulse. Fred, of course, loved it, and he and Josie decided to name the puppet Daniel in recognition of Dorothy's last name. Little did Dorothy know the part that puppet would play in Fred's life and in the lives of all those his work would touch, beginning with the very first episode of *Mister Rogers' Neighborhood*. Her gift soon became woven into God's plan for Fred.

I experienced my own divine gift when a friend gave me *Listening Below the Noise: The Transformative Power of Silence* by Anne D. LeClaire that chronicles the author's seventeen-year practice of biweekly days of silence. My friend had stumbled upon it at her favorite thrift store and immediately thought of the work my husband and I do at the Sanctuary. After reading the book herself, she felt compelled to give it to me.

As often happens when God is at work, the book arrived at the perfect time. In that season, the Spirit was leading me to go even deeper into the practice of silence and I was in the final stages of preparing to lead a silent retreat. With the retreat just a week away, God sent me the best resource for taking the next steps on my spiritual journey.

This experience and the story of Fred's tiger puppet impressed on me the importance of listening for those nudges from the Spirit, whether He stirs us to pick up a specific gift for a friend, send someone an encouraging text, or attend an event we're not sure we would feel totally comfortable at. These impulses might just be supernatural promptings, so don't shrug them off. You never know what role your gifts, words, or presence might play in someone else's life and purpose.

JOURNAL

- What resources has God miraculously brought across your path during your giant journey?

ILLUMINATED THROUGH ART

When I became acquainted with Lilias Trotter, I was a busy mother of three and a minister's wife. One might rightly ask what a single woman from a wealthy London family, who lived among the poor of Algeria more than one hundred years ago, could possibly say to me. As it turned out, a great deal!

Her insights, based on the eternal verities of Scripture and tempered with hard-won life experience, cut through current trends of thought to the very essence of my soul. They had the ring of truth, and I couldn't get enough of her practical perspective. She wrote of discouragement, struggle, perseverance, joy, love, prayer, power, weakness, and just about every other topic that mattered to me from God's point of view. She illuminated many of these truths with exquisite watercolor paintings.

She became a mentor to me, fleshing out the truth in my daily life. I wanted to find everything she wrote or painted and share my discoveries with others. Thus began a quest that eventually led to writing her biography and consulting for the documentary film about her life.

—Miriam Huffman Rockness, author of *A Passion for the Impossible and Images of Faith* and consultant on the film *Many Beautiful Things* (Giant: Lilias Trotter, missionary, artist, 1853–1928)

CAUTION SIGNS

Taking time and going slow nurtures, or as he liked to say, "nour-ishes."

—AMY HOLLINGSWORTH, *The Simple Faith of Mister Rogers*

Slowing down is something our world needs now more than ever. Busyness is a constant temptation. Whether you have kids to raise, a business to run, or a wide social circle to manage, life can keep you breathless. But when we halt our frenetic pace, we can return to our senses, identify needed adjustments, and reconnect with our Creator and ourselves.

Fred understood this principle, which is why he began every episode of *Mister Rogers' Neighborhood* by zooming in on a flashing yellow traffic light on the wall—a daily reminder to all those watching, young and old, to slow down. He knew that stillness restores our spirits, calms our minds, and even heals our bodies, because it is in the stillness that God does His best work in us.

My family, sadly, has experienced the downsides of neglecting still-ness. For my in-laws, the consequences were especially severe. Scars from childhood abuse and decades of overcommitment had taken their toll on both of them. The nonstop responsibilities of juggling bills, rais-ing kids, and serving in the church finally proved to be too much. Good judgment was pushed aside, and a messy affair destroyed two families.

Years later, when I asked my father-in-law what he would have done differently, he paused and then said, "We should have put everything on hold. I should have taken a leave from work, found someone to care for the kids, grabbed Joan's* hand, and disappeared. We should have stopped everything and figured things out, because nothing mattered more than that."

Caught up in busyness, noise, and other relationships, my in-laws lost their way. Not slowing down cost them everything.

I'm still working on the practice of slowing down in my life, but having Fred as a model of how to live at a slower pace has been a gift. Like caution signs on the side of the road, the lessons from our giants' lives can serve as warnings and rescue us from dangerous edges we're teetering on. If we heed it, their wisdom can save not only us but also those we love from great pain.

JOURNAL

- What caution sign from your giant's life has rescued you from a dangerous edge you were teetering on?

---

* Name changed for privacy purposes.

DIVINE APPOINTMENTS

Coincidence is God's way of remaining anonymous.

—Author Unknown

Divine appointments can change your life forever. Two such appointments came for Fred during his sophomore year of college. At Dartmouth College, he was majoring in Romance languages in preparation for becoming an international diplomat. Even though Dartmouth was an Ivy League school that promised an exceptional education, it couldn't have been a poorer fit. The college was large, with a reputation as a party school, and Fred was miserable there.

Halfway through his sophomore year, Fred realized that his strongest passion was music. In a seemingly ordinary conversation with music professor Arnold Kvam, the trajectory of Fred's life changed. Knowing that Dartmouth's music program wouldn't be developed enough during Fred's four years there, Kvam advised him to visit the school that he had just been recruited from: Rollins College.

Rollins was in Winter Park, Florida, the town where the Rogers family wintered during Fred's growing-up years. When Fred visited the school over Dartmouth's spring break, he was met at the airport by a group of students assigned to entertain him for the weekend. One of the students packed into the sedan that picked him up was a spunky young musician named Joanne Byrd. She would later become Mrs. Fred Rogers. Clearly, grand changes were on the horizon already.

Just as happened for Fred, life-altering moments can strike when we least expect them. And the giant journey can be full of them. I experienced one such moment myself while on vacation, near the end of my yearlong journey with Fred.

I didn't even think to investigate any connection to Fred while in Florida with family. But my ears perked up when I overheard someone mention Winter Park, and I discovered it was close by. I arranged a visit and stumbled upon a Fred Rogers walking tour that very afternoon, which felt like a divine appointment.

We began the tour by walking down Main Street toward Rollins College, listening as our guide shared stories about Fred and his time there. And as we strolled the corridors where Fred had walked more than fifty years earlier, visited the lunchroom where he first met with the music director, and stood outside his dorm, I was surprised at how moved I was.

When we reached the left side of the chapel, the guide led us to a bronze sculpture of Fred seated and surrounded by children touching him and looking up at him. Fred, with crow's feet and a twinkle in his eyes, looked back at them, his love somehow transmitted through the bronze. To my amazement, the guide informed us that the sculpture had just been unveiled the day before. Fred's son, mentors, and colleagues from *Mister Rogers' Neighborhood* had all been there for the dedication.

I slowly walked around the sculpture, wishing I had hours to look at it. As I studied the intricate details, I noticed our guide waving me over. He tilted his head toward another group and whispered, "I think that is the sculptor right there."

Then, with the time of our tour just about up, our guide led us to the music performance building. We could see motion inside. When we opened the door, a greeter asked if we were there for the lecture. It turned out that Paul Day, the sculptor, was speaking in fifteen minutes!

Divine appointments like these are no accident. We can't always comprehend how God lines up the circumstances so perfectly or understand in the moment the reasons certain things happen the way they do. Often we don't even realize we're walking into one of these appointments until a heavenly glow overshadows a regular event. They can change the course of our lives in a way God has always intended, leaving us in a wake of wonder at His incredible gift of love.

JOURNAL

- What large or small divine appointments have you experienced on the journey with your giant?

PILGRIMAGE PRINCIPLE

NOTICE GOD BESIDE YOU

....

All at once their eyes were opened and they realized he was Jesus! Then suddenly, in a flash, Jesus vanished from before their eyes! Stunned, they looked at each other and said, "Why didn't we recognize him? Didn't our hearts burn with the flames of holy passion while we walked beside him? He unveiled for us such profound revelation from the Scriptures!"

—Luke 24:31–32, TPT

You don't always have a choice of whom you're going to sleep next to when you arrive late at the albergue. Last night, you were one of the last. You've been doing your best to tend to your weary muscles, but the tendonitis in your shins has been excruciating. You've lost five days already, resting in Pamplona, Burgos, León, Astorga, and Sarria. The Camino family you started with in Saint Jean is probably in Santiago already.

As the host leads you to the dormitory, you discover that it is nothing more than a large attic with sleeping bags on the floor—one right next to the other on each side of a narrow room with an aisle down the middle. Even so, you are thankful for a place to sleep. You pray that the pilgrim next to you will be someone quiet, but then a large man swings open the bathroom door, walks over to the sleeping bag beside you, and plops down.

After you exchange greetings, he turns to his companions and begins bantering loudly with them. As their conversation stretches on for what seems like an eternity, you try to reassure yourself: *You can do this. It's just one night.*

Despite the late night, you wake up early and are relieved that your new friend isn't stirring yet. You manage to get on the trail well ahead of him and his talkative companions. But as you slowly make your way forward, trying not to aggravate your sensitive shins, the pain returns halfway through the morning. Hobbling through the streets, with each step sending shooting pain up your leg, you don't know how you will make it the next albergue.

Then you hear a voice behind you saying, "Oh, it's the American." It's him.

To your surprise, he notices your limp and stops to chat. As he pulls a roll of athletic tape out of his pack, he explains that he is a physical therapist. After tightly wrapping your shins, he takes your pack and carries it all the way to the next town. He even stays with you until you get safely settled in your albergue. As he waves goodbye, you realize you never even got his name. Nonetheless, the divine appointment brings tears to your eyes. This attention from a stranger is the most profound kindness you've ever experienced—an expression of God's love through human hands as He watches over every step you take.*

• • •

You never know how or when God is going to show up and walk right beside you. On a pilgrimage, in life, and on the giant journey there are moments when the invisible God becomes visible through another person. It might be only afterward that you notice it was the presence of God appearing in a way you hadn't expected, maybe even through the care of a stranger. With all the tough moments on the journey, these moments are especially sweet.

JOURNAL

- When have you experienced God walking beside you on the journey?

---

* *Walking the Camino: Six Ways to Santiago*, directed by Lydia B. Smith, 2013.

MILE MARKER

The giant journey offers natural moments to pause at the side of the trail. Take time to do this at the end of each month.

FINAL STEPS ON THE TRAIL

People often ask if there is a quicker way to walk with a giant. Of course, there is. You could walk with a giant for a month, ninety days, or half a year and still benefit. But as in other areas of life, the richer rewards usually come after longer periods of time. Now that you've been on the journey for almost a year—planting, weeding, and watering—the harvest is ready. And now you get to gather it in.

- Settle beside a window or outside where you can look out over the natural world and take some time to prayerfully reflect on the harvest of your journey.
- With the Lord's guidance, journal about the ways you've changed, the moments when you saw growth in your relationship with God and others, the steps you've taken in pursuing your purpose, and the good that has happened in the world because of your transformation.

REFLECTION

Take some time to reflect on the following questions as you wrap up the month. Your answers can be great indicators of what the Spirit might be leading you to focus on in the month ahead.

Summary: What direction did the Lord take you this month? Did your month go like you thought it would? Were there any unexpected leadings, twists, or turns?

Growth: In what areas of your life do you see growth or shifts in your thinking?

Excitement: When you think about your journey, what fills you with energy?

Challenges: What is bothering you? Do you have any unanswered questions or frustrations related to your journey?

PILGRIM PRAYER

Jesus, You tell us that You no longer call us servants but instead friends. I'll never comprehend how this can be. But, Jesus, my friend, thank You for walking beside me. Open my eyes to those You send as messengers of Your love, just as You opened the eyes of Your early followers on the road to Emmaus. Use me as You will to be that kind of messenger for others. Open my eyes to Your movements in my life. I'm watching. Amen.

TRAVELOGUE

GLIMPSE THE FULL PICTURE

Medieval pilgrims displayed qualities I wanted to emulate. They were patient. Faithful. Courageous. And inefficient—gloriously so. Pilgrims were in it for the long haul. They risked everything to take a journey of faith. And the conviction that drove them is one to which I daily aspire.

—LISA DEAM, *3000 Miles to Jesus*

STEPS ALONG THE TRAIL

As you near the end of your journey, consider these possible focus points for month 11:

☐ Fill in the gaps in your understanding of your giant's life by savoring pictures, quotes, podcasts, or documentaries about them. Pay attention to what moves you, recognizing that the Spirit might be stirring in an area where He wants to work.

☐ Look back at the list you made in month 9 and choose a topic that you would like to dig deeper into before the journey is done.

☐ Reflecting on last month's Pilgrimage Principle, consider writing a thank-you letter or taking a meal to someone who became the hands of Jesus to you on your journey. Or invite a friend to lunch to share with them about what you've been learning from your giant.

☐ Remember that God has invited you on a unique journey. Don't worry if none of these ideas resonate with you. Just stay attuned to how the Spirit is guiding you.

☐ Complete the weekly journal prompts and the trail guide.

 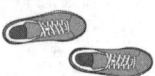

JOURNEY WITH FRED

Check out these resources if you're joining the giant journey with Mister Rogers:

- *Mister Rogers' Neighborhood: A Visual History* by Melissa Wagner, Tim Lybarger, and Jenna McGuiggan
- *Welcome to the Neighborhood: A Mister Rogers Tribute Podcast* hosted by Rick Lee James
- *Mister Rogers and Me* documentary by Benjamin Wagner and Christofer Wagner

TRAIL GUIDE

Focus: What is your primary focus for this month? How is God directing your journey?

Media: What are you reading, watching, or listening to as you engage with your giant this month?

Quotes: What meaningful quotes would you like to remember from this month?

Experiences: What new places, activities, or events are you experiencing this month because of your giant?

Faith: In what ways has your giant drawn you closer to God this month? What spiritual practices have you engaged in as a result of your giant journey?

Sticky Points: What questions or topics might you want to explore more later?

MISSION STATEMENT

I've met a lot of interesting people. I've met great actors. I've met
great writers. I've met great this, great that. But Fred's the only person that I would call a great man.

—Tom Junod, in *The Good Neighbor* by Maxwell King

Tom Junod, a career journalist, traveled the world and interviewed
countless influential people. Yet no one had quite the impact on
him that Fred Rogers did. The friendship that developed between
them was so striking that it was the subject of the 2019 film *A Beautiful
Day in the Neighborhood*. Incredibly, Junod's experience wasn't singular.
Many others described being similarly transformed through their relationship with Fred.

After my tour of Rollins College, I found myself processing Fred's
impact on my life. How had God used him to shape me in the last ten
months? What had been God's plan in leading me to Fred in the first
place?

Circling back to my initial notes about the journey, I was reminded of
one of the primary goals I had written down after deciding to walk with
Fred: "To become as loving as he was—Jesus to so many." I thought
back over the last several weeks and months. In what ways had my ca-
pacity to love increased? Could I point to any specific examples where I
was becoming more like Jesus? Had I learned, like Fred, to serve well
and love deeply in my neighborhood?

Fred once described the message he most wanted his life to convey:

As human beings, our job in life is to help people realize how rare and valuable each one of us really is, that each of us has something that no one else has—or ever will have—something inside that is unique to all time. It's our job to encourage each other to discover that uniqueness and to provide ways of developing its expression.*

In his last conversation with author, reporter, and close friend Amy Hollingsworth, Fred added to the above statement by saying,

[I want others to know] that they are loved by the Person who created them, in a unique way.

If they could know that . . . they could look [at] their neighbor and realize, "My neighbor has unique value too." . . . If they could value that person—if they could love that person—in ways that we know that the Eternal loves us, then I would be very grateful.†

As I reflected on my year with Fred, I realized that's exactly what his life had spoken to me. Furthermore, if I were to define what I believe God offers us through our giant journey, I can't think of more beautiful description than an adaptation of Fred's life message:

The gift of knowing they are loved by the eternal God who created them. Of realizing how rare and valuable each one of us really is. Of seeing how each one of us has gifts no one else has or ever will have. And of discovering, in walking with their giant, their uniqueness and the freedom and empowerment to bring the full expression of that uniqueness to the world for the glory of God.

Fred's life and mission statement revealed something deeper that God was inviting me to uncover—not just for my own benefit, but for

---

* Fred Rogers, *You Are Special: Neighborly Words of Wisdom from Mister Rogers* (Penguin, 1995), 12.

† Amy Hollingsworth, *The Simple Faith of Mister Rogers: Spiritual Insights from the World's Most Beloved Neighbor* (Thomas Nelson, 2005), 161.

the benefit of those around me as well. The same is true for you too. When a lesson from your giant or an aspect of their life sparks a shift in your soul, know that God is the one igniting the spark. He knows what messages you need to hear, and—just as He speaks through His Word, prayer, and creation—He might use the life of your giant to spur you on toward the purpose He has for you.

JOURNAL

- What powerful reasons are you seeing for why God might have led you to your giant?

IN THE BLINK OF AN EYE

I am not in control. I am not in a hurry. I walk in faith and hope. I greet everyone with peace. I bring back only what God gives me.

—MURRAY BODO, "The Pilgrim's Credo"

As much as we want good things to last forever, the preciousness of life or a pilgrimage lies in the fact that there is a beginning and an end. All our journeys are fleeting. Even Fred faced some anxiety about his journey being done as he neared the end of his life.

In February 2003, as his cancer progressed and he realized his days on earth were coming to a close, he asked his wife, Joanne, if he had done enough with his gifts during his life. With profound love in her eyes, she assured him that if anyone had lived to the fullest and served others well, it was him.

Many pilgrims that travel the Camino wish for a few more days before they have to say goodbye to new friends and to the journey itself. They dreamed, planned, and trained for it for so long. As they reach the end, they wonder how many of their hopes for their pilgrimage were actually fulfilled. Did they meet enough pilgrims or the right ones? Did they experience Spain, the people, and the culture like they dreamed they would? Did they grow spiritually like they wanted to? Did they come to know themselves at a deeper level like they hoped?

You may soon be asking similar questions about the journey with your giant. With so little time left, you may open one book and then wonder if you should be spending your time in another. You may worry that you won't have time for everything. You may feel the pressure to make sure you get to the crux—the essence of the transformation you hoped this journey would bring.

Resist this temptation. Stacking anxiety on top of your expectations will only stifle your growth and make you feel paralyzed. Instead of stressing about the moments ticking by or letting anxiety steal your joy and spontaneity, live in the truth that God is holding all of it, remind yourself of all the incredible things He has done so far, and walk the rest of the journey as a curious child instead of a controlling adult. Remain in the present, wake up with joy, and receive what each day brings.

May the Lord help you trust and rest. Right now, it can be difficult to see all the good things that are happening. But when you look back, you'll see how perfectly God orchestrated all of it. The beautiful truth is that when you finish your giant journey or fly home from your pilgrimage, God's work isn't done; it's just shifting.

JOURNAL

- How are you feeling about the time you have left on the journey?

FOLLOWING A FREEDOM FIGHTER

Harriet Tubman has always had my attention, but then I started following the Community Healing Network through their Emotional Emancipation Summits during the Congressional Black Caucus conference at the D.C. convention center. They were remarkable events.

In 2019, we gathered in Richmond to remember the arrival of the first slave ship in Yorktown. In March of that year, I led a pilgrimage to Virginia's Eastern Shore for the Shalem Institute for Spiritual Formation with a historian friend who had walked the entire Underground Railroad. Then the movie *Harriet* released, followed by the movie *Just Mercy,* followed in turn by a pilgrimage that another Shalem member and I took to Alabama. It was led by an Episcopal woman, Dr. Catherine Meeks, and it was powerful!

With no solicitation from me, I received a call from Broadleaf Books' senior editor inviting me to write a book without specifying a particular topic. I said I wanted to write about Harriet's intimate relationship with the Divine and how she demonstrated for me internalized freedom.

—Therese Taylor-Stinson, spiritual director, author of *Walking the Way of Harriet Tubman: Public Mystic and Freedom Fighter* (Giant: Harriet Tubman, abolitionist, freedom fighter, 1820–1913)

WEEK THREE

HABITS OF LOVE

....

L'essentiel est invisible pour les yeux.

—ANTOINE DE SAINT-EXUPÉRY, *The Little Prince*

"What is essential is invisible to the eye."
This statement from *The Little Prince* was one of Fred's life principles and a favorite quote that hung on a wall in his office. As important as his visible work was—nine hundred episodes of *Mister Rogers' Neighborhood*, hundreds of speeches and songs, and much more—just as important to Fred was the work that wasn't seen, such as the thousands of letters he wrote throughout his lifetime.

Letters came from fans who watched him on television (not just children and teens but their parents, too), family members who had accompanied guests on *Mister Rogers' Neighborhood*, reporters who had interviewed him, professors he had taken classes from, and even his lifelong love, Joanne. Starting with the letter he wrote her in 1951, asking her to marry him, Fred and Joanne exchanged many letters throughout their marriage.

Fred viewed each letter as a sacred trust and wrote back to each sender, many times tucking in a little something extra, like an article that "made me think of you," a picture he'd snapped during their time together and signed on the back, or a special trinket. His letters weren't always long. Sometimes they were just a few sentences. But countless people became his pen pals and continued to correspond with him through the years, some even until his passing. Many of those pen pals still treasure his letters today.

One letter was written to a young boy named Tommy, who faced challenging health issues during his too-short life. Tommy died a few days after getting Fred's letter, but not before he wrote Mister Rogers a thank-you to tell him how much he had liked the record album Fred had sent and how his "I.V. doesn't hurt just a little when they put it in."

After Tommy's death, his mom wrote to Fred, recalling her son's joy at receiving the letter and record even as she processed the grief and bitterness in her own heart. In both correspondences, Mister Rogers took the time to care, to listen, and to love. Who can estimate what his letters meant to that little boy, his mother, and the thousands of others who received them?

In 1975, it was estimated that *Mister Rogers' Neighborhood* was receiving fifteen thousand letters a year. The Fred Rogers Institute in Latrobe has since archived more than thirty-six thousand notes and letters.* Yet somehow, even with the media's insatiable appetite to publicize every bit of a famous person's life, these letters remain virtually invisible, illustrating the truth that "what is essential is invisible to the eye." I imagine Fred would be very glad about that.

Fred's habit of sharing love through letters spoke volumes to me as I recently considered the little pile of letters on my desk: one from a young friend with whom I've developed a fun and playful correspondence; another containing our family "letter circle" that travels among the dozen or so older and younger women in our family; some from directees to whom I offer companionship by mail; and others from our three Compassion children, whom we will most likely never meet in person. I love this stack of letters and the people who penned the words, whose hands tucked the letters into the envelopes, and whose spirits are with me as I read and write back. Learning about Fred's thousands of letters inspired me anew, and I pray that my little stack will be like his.

---

* Court Mann, "*The Many, Many, Many Letters of Mister Rogers,*" *Deseret News*, October 21, 2020, www.deseret.com/entertainment/2020/10/21/21189417/mister-rogers-neighborhood -fred-letters-viewer-mail-correspondence-archive-religion-education-where.

JOURNAL

- What habit of love has your giant inspired or strengthened in your life?

SHOWN HOW TO LIVE

I've been journeying with Dr. Howard Thurman for many years. I was introduced to his teachings in the nineties when I heard a priest mention him as Martin Luther King, Jr.'s spiritual mentor. I immediately went out and bought a book of his writings and was blown away. The words on the pages spoke to the deepest part of my being.

I still have that book and continue to refer to it. Dr. Thurman's spirituality helped me make sense of my own spiritual journey. Always a seeker open to exploring different traditions, I felt out of step with those around me. However, Dr. Thurman's spirituality encouraged me to be open and seek the Divine wherever I found myself. He helped me understand my experience of God in nature. Early on in life I learned to treasure the many hours spent in the rolling hills of the Shenandoah Valley, my boyhood sanctuary. Dr. Thurman's beliefs about the centrality of religious experience helped me make sense of the burning bush moment I experienced in the woods as a teenager.

Through Dr. Thurman, I now realize that Jesus is the center of it all and God is the goal.

—Phillip Johnson, psychologist (Giant: Howard Thurman, writer, theologian, civil rights leader, 1899–1981)

THE GIFT OF A NEW PERSPECTIVE

Although Abel is long dead, he still speaks to us by his example of faith.

—Hebrews 11:4, NLT

One of the greatest gifts we can receive from our giants is a new perspective. I experienced this firsthand while listening to an episode of Rick Lee James's *Welcome to the Neighborhood* podcast in which he interviewed Tim Madigan, the author of *I'm Proud of You*. The new perspective I gained turned out to be lifechanging for one of my closest relationships.

Tim and Fred first met in 1995 when Tim traveled to Pittsburgh to interview Fred. After the interview, Fred became a faithful friend. The two of them exchanged many letters and emails throughout their seven-and-a-half-year friendship. At the end of every letter, Fred would always include the words "I'm proud of you."

But because of his messy relationship with his father, Tim doubted Fred's unconditional love and was sure that some failure or character flaw of his would eventually cause Fred to turn away from him. When he asked his wife for a divorce, he was convinced the end of Fred's unconditional love had come. After all, how could Fred still be proud of him after such a heartbreaking failure?

When Tim wrote to Fred to tell him the news, he fully expected rejection. But instead, he received a letter full of compassion and signed with a promise that nothing would ever change Fred's love for him. No matter what Tim ever said or did, Fred would always be proud of him.*

As I listened to this story, I thought about my sister. Her marriage had also been messy. She had tried everything to fix it for twenty-two years and then couldn't try anymore. So she decided to end it.

My sister and I had always been extremely close. On top of being sisters, we share the special bond of twinhood. We know each other's thoughts and can just about finish each other's sentences. We have the same laugh and the same nose. No matter how long it's been since we've been together, we can pick up where we left off like no time has passed.

But our relationship reached a tipping point when she moved toward divorce. After living through twenty-five years of shrapnel, pain, and tears since my in-laws' marriage blew apart, I wanted to spare my sister from similar trauma. We had many conversations. I tried to reason with her. But she had already decided what she was going to do. She didn't expect me to understand or God to excuse her actions, but she knew He would forgive her and believed her story would have a happy ending.

My experience shouted otherwise. I kept trying to make her see the situation the way I saw it, until finally she told me that if I didn't promise not to talk about it again, she was going to cut me out of her life. I couldn't promise that. So she severed ties.

We talked a handful of times in the ten years apart. I missed her like crazy and prayed for restoration, but it never came.

Then, when I heard Tim's story again on the podcast, my eyes were suddenly opened. I recognized how badly I'd hurt my sister. I felt compelled to apologize, so I wrote her a letter. When it arrived, she thought it was a Christmas card and set it aside for a quieter moment in January. When she finally opened it more than a month later, she sent me a text.

---

* Rick Lee James, host, *Welcome to the Neighborhood: A Mister Rogers Tribute Podcast*, episode 35, "Welcome to the Neighborhood: A Mister Rogers Tribute Podcast with Guest Tim Madigan," April 30, 2021, https://rickleejames.substack.com/p/welcome-to-the-neighborhood-a-mister-5c8.

The note had meant the world to her, and she was open to repairing our relationship.

That was it. That was what we needed. Through the years, I'd shed buckets of tears and begged God to show us a different way. I'd studied the Bible, attended church, met with my spiritual director, and gone on retreats, but restoration hadn't come. Until that day, when God used the story of a faithful follower of Christ, my spiritual giant, who, though dead, "still speaks to us by his example of faith."

And I got my sister back!

JOURNAL

- How has walking with your giant had a positive impact on important relationships in your life?

PILGRIMAGE PRINCIPLE

LOOK AROUND FOR HELP

Two are better than one,
  because they have a good return for their labor:
If either of them falls down,
  one can help the other up.
But pity anyone who falls
  and has no one to help them up.

—Ecclesiastes 4:9–10

You've been on the trail for weeks. Things have been going well. You've been following the map and making turns at all the yellow flechas, which have led you from one town to another. But then you notice that it's been longer than usual since you've seen a yellow arrow. Or another pilgrim. In fact, you don't see anyone ahead of or behind you.

Confused, you pull out your map. But as your anxiety increases, you find it difficult to make sense of all the lines and markings, especially with only an hour of daylight left.

You walk down the street, only to turn around and walk back. When you reach the crossroads where you discovered you were off course, you look up and see a middle-aged man walking toward you. Maybe he's used to seeing disoriented pilgrims if he lives this close to the Camino.

"Hola. ¿Puedo ayudarte?" he asks. "Hello. Can I help you?"

"I've gotten off course, and I can't figure out how to get back," you say.

He takes your map and, pointing down the road, says in English, "Walk down the road three blocks, and then turn left. Go four blocks more, and then you'll see a coffee shop across the street and a bridge . . ."

He trails off as he notes the growing panic on your face. Offering a friendly smile, he says, "I have time. Would you like me to take you?"

You breathe a sigh of relief. "That would be awesome."

• • •

Sometimes on pilgrimage, even with the best maps or GPS to guide you, you might still need another human being to help you get back on course. Someone who knows the way from personal experience and can guide you on your path forward.

Our life in Christ is the same. We can know what the Bible says and even memorize long passages from it, but when it comes to living out what Scripture teaches, we may need more than just words on a page. Think about it: No one knew the Torah better than the religious leaders who lived strictly by the text of the law but often missed the spirit of it.

Thankfully, God hasn't sent us on our journey alone. When we get tangled up trying to figure out how to understand what we read in the Bible and how to live according to God's plan, half the journey is putting our heads down to study His Word and pray. But the other half is lifting our heads and looking around for those trusted guides that He has provided to show us how to live well.

JOURNAL

- How has your giant shown you a new way to live out your faith in an area where you have been stuck?

MILE MARKER

The giant journey offers natural moments to pause at the side of the trail. Take time to do this at the end of each month.

FINAL STEPS ON THE TRAIL

Slip away for some time alone with the Father. After a month of savoring the journey, how does your heart feel?

- After reviewing your notes and resources from this month, make a list of three to five things (quotes, pictures, podcasts, documentaries, etc.) that powerfully moved you.
- With that list in front of you, sit quietly for five to fifteen minutes, asking the Lord what He wants to reveal to you. As you listen, write in your journal what you sense Him saying to you.
- Even if you don't hear anything, simply enjoy His presence, knowing that He is filling every part of you, bringing healing and peace.

REFLECTION

Take some time to reflect on the following questions as you wrap up the month. Your answers can be great indicators of what the Spirit might be leading you to focus on in the month ahead.

Summary: What direction did the Lord take you this month? Did your month go like you thought it would? Were there any unexpected leadings, twists, or turns?

Growth: In what areas of your life do you see growth or shifts in your thinking?

Excitement: When you think about your journey, what fills you with energy?

Challenges: What is bothering you? Do you have any unanswered questions or frustrations related to your journey?

PILGRIM PRAYER

Oh God, as I spend this time in Your presence, I'm astounded that You have given human beings this ability to know You—to hear Your voice, feel Your love, and sense You moving inside us. Reflecting on the ways You have been working in my life makes me want to open myself even further to You. As I savor what You're doing in me and the steps I'm taking forward in my purpose, most of all I'm savoring You—Father, Son, and Holy Spirit. Growing closer to You is my greatest treasure. Amen.

TRAVELOGUE

THE FINAL TOAST

There is a time for everything . . .
a time to weep and a time to laugh,
a time to mourn and a time to dance. . . .
He has made everything beautiful in its time.

—Ecclesiastes 3:1, 4, 11

STEPS ALONG THE TRAIL

You've almost made it! This month, you will be not only walking the final miles with your giant but enjoying a meaningful final reflection as well. As you celebrate the home stretch, consider these possible focus points:

☐ As you treasure the last miles of your journey, try out a new activity connected to one of your giant's strengths. What would a final toast with your giant look like?

☐ If there is a holiday this month, ask the Lord how you might combine your holiday observation with your giant journey. Follow any ideas that come to mind.

☐ Spend the month reading through your notes from the year.

☐ Remember that God has invited you on a unique journey. Don't worry if none of these ideas resonate with you. Just stay attuned to how the Spirit is guiding you.

☐ Complete the weekly journal prompts and the trail guide.

JOURNEY WITH FRED

Check out these resources if you're joining the giant journey with Mister Rogers:

- *It's You I Like: A Star-Studded Tribute to America's Favorite Neighbor*, PBS
- *The Giving Box: Create a Tradition of Giving with Your Children* by Fred Rogers
- *Dear Mister Rogers, Does It Ever Rain in Your Neighborhood? Letters to Mister Rogers* by Fred Rogers
- *Mister Rogers' Neighborhood: A Visual History* by Melissa Wagner, Tim Lybarger, and Jenna McGuiggan

TRAIL GUIDE

Focus: What is your primary focus for this month? How is God directing your journey?

Media: What are you reading, watching, or listening to as you engage with your giant this month?

Quotes: What meaningful quotes would you like to remember from this month?

Experiences: What new places, activities, or events are you experiencing this month because of your giant?

Faith: In what ways has your giant drawn you closer to God this month? What spiritual practices have you engaged in as a result of your giant journey?

Sticky Points: What questions or topics might you want to explore more later?

ENDING WELL

....

To finish the moment, to find the journey's end in every step of the road, to live the greatest number of good hours, is wisdom.

—RALPH WALDO EMERSON, "Experience"

As you enter the final stage of the journey, think back on the miles you've traveled, the lessons you've learned, and the challenges you've navigated. Allow yourself to breathe in the delight of this moment and the triumph of the distance you've come. Then think about the celebratory way you would like to finish. Consider what a final toast with your giant would look like.

For example, if your giant is someone who was gifted in hospitality, you might connect with friends over coffee or dinner, or you could read a book of simple hospitality practices that you could implement after the journey is done. If your giant was more interested in enjoying God's creation, perhaps you could spend time in your garden or pick up a book of nature poetry.

Because my journey with Fred ended in December, I ordered *The Giving Box,* a book Fred wrote about generosity. I also planned to flip through *Mister Rogers' Neighborhood: A Visual History* and put together a collage of pictures that especially tugged on my heart.

But even with this plan in place, I still felt like I was missing something. After suiting up in my snow pants, I headed outside for a moonlit walk. My thoughts began swirling around Advent, and I asked the Lord how I could draw closer to Him during this holy season. I wondered how I might combine Advent with my giant journey and how Mister Rogers might celebrate Advent.

I envisioned him loving the people in his neighborhood and attending the services in his Presbyterian church as well as the candlelight services at Saint Vincent Archabbey. If his community had a Christmas tree lighting, I imagined him bundling up in his wool coat, scarf, mittens, and earmuffs and drinking hot cocoa with his neighbors. I could just about hear him gasp in the magical moment when the tree lights came on for the first time.

That was it! I would celebrate Advent in community.

For me, this was a significant point of growth. My normal pattern in December was to cocoon myself in my home, welcome my family for Christmas traditions, and participate only in my home church's festivities. But after hearing this quiet instruction from the Holy Spirit, I remembered the Christmas tree lighting in our rural hometown and that a friend had invited me to an Advent celebration at her church. Following in Mister Rogers's footsteps, I decided to accept her invitation.

Even when we might be tempted to isolate ourselves or maintain our comfortable routines, the Holy Spirit often nudges us through our giants to expand our lives in meaningful ways. I couldn't think of a better final toast with Fred than to broaden the borders of my neighborhood and open my heart to celebrate Advent with others in my community.

JOURNAL

- How is the Lord leading you to savor this last month of your journey?

- What would a final toast with your giant look like?

THE POWER OF CONNECTION

Mister Rogers built his life around the notion that human connection would lead to understanding, and from there to kindness and generosity.

—GAVIN EDWARDS, *Kindness and Wonder*

In 1969, Mister Rogers invited Officer Clemmons to sit with him by a kiddie swimming pool for a revolutionary episode of *Mister Rogers' Neighborhood*. After taking off their shoes and socks, they immersed their feet in the cool water. When they were done, Mister Rogers dried Officer Clemmons's feet with a towel.

Although this may not seem like a big deal today, Fred's actions were revolutionary for that time. After all, Officer Clemmons was Black, Martin Luther King, Jr., had been assassinated a year earlier, and racial tensions in the United States were at their peak. Even though the Civil Rights Act of 1964 had outlawed segregation, many facilities—including restaurants, hotels, and movie theaters—had been slow to comply. In fact, some of the most violent protests occurred on desegregated beaches and at public swimming pools.

In that single episode, Mister Rogers, through his quiet example, taught his viewers—children and adults alike—that one of the greatest weapons for breaking down the walls of racism is to spend time with those who are different from you.

With this story at the forefront of my mind, I accepted a friend's invitation to join her at an event at her church, which was a different denomination from mine. Four denominations had come together to host the event in an effort to provide a space to mix with others of different races and faith perspectives. A Catholic man served as the moderator, while the other hosts were Presbyterian, Lutheran, and Episcopal ministers and a Hispanic woman who worked with the homeless.

As the panel introduced themselves, I realized that the group had different political beliefs than I did. Clearly, I was surrounded by people who saw the world through very different glasses from mine! Yet their desire to live like Christ and to do good resonated deeply with me.

When it was time for our table discussion, I was assigned to a table of people all in their fifties and sixties. Straying off our assigned question, my tablemates asked about my faith and what had brought me to the event. More than keeping to the agenda, they were interested in knowing who I was as a person, and I felt the same about them.

Later, the panel talked about how often we see Christ not in the grand, extravagant things but in the ordinary. Sharing the experience that evening with the people around my table was a clear example of this. Though we may not have been from the same economic, religious, racial, or political circles, spending a few hours with one another broke down the walls that divided us and helped us see one another not as opponents but as brothers and sisters in Christ.

With his powerful message of neighborliness, Fred inspired me to look beyond my immediate circle to those I may never have spent time with before. In the same way, your giant may challenge you to connect with brothers and sisters you might otherwise never have the privilege of meeting. These connections clear our clouded vision and enable us to understand one another better, bringing about healing, growth, and life-giving change.

JOURNAL

- How has your giant helped you connect with brothers and sisters in Christ from different economic, religious, racial, or political circles?

HEARING JESUS THROUGH MY GIANT

My spiritual giant was Desmond Tutu. I intentionally chose him because he is not a white European. I wanted to choose someone different from me. As a Black South African, he knew great suffering and great joy.

One of the things he wrote about has stayed with me in my spiritual direction ministry: Our role is to be listeners to those entrusted to our care. We are to be "midwives of meaning" as we listen to our directees' stories and help them sense and experience the presence of the Holy Spirit in their lives. We help them "give birth" to whatever God is calling them to.

Desmond Tutu always sought to hear Jesus's voice guiding him. That has been an inspiration to me personally and in the ministry of spiritual direction I am called to.

—Gail Gunst Heffner, professor emerita, spiritual director (Giant: Desmond Tutu, Anglican bishop, civil rights activist, 1931–2021)

LOVE YOUR NEIGHBOR

"A Neighbor," Mister Rogers said, "is whoever you happen to be with at the moment," and then added, "especially if that person is in need."

—AMY HOLLINGSWORTH, *The Simple Faith of Mister Rogers*

The word *neighbor* was extremely important to Fred. Everything from his daily interactions with strangers to his life's work on *Mister Rogers' Neighborhood* emphasized his greatest priority: being there for those around him—his neighbors—especially in their times of great pain.

More than once, when Fred would learn that a child who watched him on television was facing a surgery or terminal illness, he would get on a plane to be by their bedside and comfort their hurting parents. Friends, co-workers, and fans were astonished at how his letters, emails, and phone calls would arrive in their moments of greatest struggle.

One of Fred's staff members, Lisa Hamilton, shared how Fred was there for her and her thirty-one-year-old husband, Scott, after they learned that he had cancer. During the eight months of his illness, Fred came often to pray with them. Then, prompted during his daily prayer time that they were in particular need, Fred miraculously showed up at their front door just minutes after Lisa had woken to find that Scott had passed on to heaven during the night.

Whether with a word, a shoulder, silence, or tears, Fred was there for his neighbors in the most agonizing periods of their lives.

Although being present to neighbors who are grieving wasn't a lesson I was eager to learn, life had other plans.

Near the end of my journey with Fred, one of the ways God led me to observe Advent in my neighborhood was to be beside a dear friend as she buried her daughter-in-law after her unexpected death. This wonderful wife and mother left behind seven children, and I had no words to offer my grieving friend. The question "Why?" remained in a vacuum of silence.

But my friend and her family didn't need words or answers. Even though I longed to do more, they were grateful I was simply there with them in their grief. As Fred knew, my presence and love for my friend, sister, and neighbor were enough.

JOURNAL

- How has your giant helped you love your neighbor?

SELF-FORGETTING GOSPEL SERVICE

George Washington Carver was born into slavery around 1864. With an exceptional intellect and fragile body, he focused on tasks using his brain instead of his physique.

Exceptional people are often terrible human beings. But George deeply loved the Lord and offered the southern economy—crumbling because of its overdependence on the cotton plant—the discoveries he believed the Lord had given him, even though he had suffered extreme prejudice from some of the very people he was helping.

He never patented any of his more than three hundred discoveries from the soybean and other plants, explaining that they were God's creations that he had no right to withhold from others.

I love him for his identity, activity, and legacy.

On his tombstone is written, "A life that stood out as a gospel of self-forgetting service. He could have added fortune to fame but caring for neither he found happiness and honor in being helpful to the world."

I want to live a life of self-forgetting gospel service. As someone who is told that he is gifted, I ask myself, *What am I doing with what I have been given? Do I use the ideas I have been given for my self-interest, status, and success or for others?*

—Sho Baraka, recording artist and author of *He Saw That It Was Good* (Giant: George Washington Carver, agricultural scientist, inventor, professor, 1864–1943)

YOUR MOST IMPORTANT NEIGHBOR

Love begins at home, and it is not how much we do, but how much love we put in the action that we do.

—MOTHER TERESA, Nobel lecture, 1979

Some moments change you forever. Journalist Tim Madigan experienced one of these moments in his first conversation with Fred. He called him for what should have been a five-minute conversation to schedule an interview, but they ended up talking for more than an hour. Eventually, Fred asked him, "Do you know the most important thing in the world to me right now?"

"No," he replied.

"Talking to Mr. Tim Madigan on the telephone," Fred said.*

This simple statement was both shocking and humbling to Tim, but it was also a poignant gift to know how Fred felt about him and their conversation.

I often need this reminder to be present to others in my own life.

Recently, I was knee deep in wrapping paper, tape, bows, and Amazon packages, with every minute scheduled to check off all the Christmas preparations before the kids arrived and the festivities began. As my husband left for work, he asked what we had going on that night.

"Nothing," I answered, wanting to keep it that way. "Why? Is there something you have in mind?"

---

* Tim Madigan, *I'm Proud of You: My Friendship with Fred Rogers* (Ubuntu, 2012), 13.

"Yes, the Smiths' small group Christmas party. It's been so long since we've been with them. I thought it would be fun to go."

Fun? Yeah, for a man without Christmas to pull off!

Maintaining outward calm, I said, "Well, maybe you could go, and I'll stay home and work on these Christmas projects."

Cool as a cucumber, he said, "Okay. We'll talk later."

Wise enough after years of marriage to know how ineffective it would be to push me, he dropped the subject and walked away, giving me the time I needed to come to my senses.

He hadn't been gone long when I remembered Fred's words to Tim. Words that had been so gripping, they were one of the first things Tim wrote about in his book about his relationship with Fred. And here they were speaking to me again, eleven months after I first read them.

I then heard the Spirit whisper, "Don't let your to-do list keep you from loving your closest neighbor. Leave the wrapping paper on the counter. Shut the door to the guest room. Don't worry about checking everything off the list. What's important is, and always will be, the person in front of you right now."

When my husband got home, I greeted him with a big kiss. I explained my change of heart, and together we enjoyed a precious evening, nibbling Christmas cookies and sitting under twinkling lights with this special group of our closest "neighbors."

If we learn anything from those who passionately follow Christ, we should learn how they loved those closest to them. Jesus modeled this for us by how He cared for His tiny band of twelve disciples, even when surrounded by thousands of others who needed His attention. Our spiritual giants teach us this lesson as well. Their example can help us to shake off our inward focus and rigid routines and give us a reminder of what's important exactly when we need it.

JOURNAL

- v your giant reminded you of what is important?

PILGRIMAGE PRINCIPLE

EXPECT MORE

....

> Oh Lord, I recognize a relentless restlessness within my soul, calling
> me onwards, upwards, and inwards to yourself. And so, I set my heart
> upon pilgrimage and my feet on the road, my hopes upon heaven, and
> my eyes upon you.
>
> —Lectio 365, 24-7Prayer.com*

There it is—Santiago! After five weeks and five hundred miles, you've made it. Finally, you're here!

There's celebrating, feasting, and taking pictures galore as you hug the other pilgrims with whom you've shared the trail. After you've walked through sunshine and rain and endured blisters and tears, your heart nearly bursts with happiness at all you've accomplished.

The celebration culminates with mass in the cathedral. Sitting there in the cool, dim interior, you take in every moment as the incense-filled urn swings in a huge arc over your head and the names of those who have completed their pilgrimage are read. It's hard to believe that you've reached your destination.

• • •

You may not have physically walked a five-hundred-mile trail in northern Spain, but you've been on a journey just as powerful. As you took your first steps twelve months ago and looked down the trail, you could only dream about where you would be today.

Think back now to the first moments when you were either nervous or excited about choosing your giant. Remember all the joys along the

---

* From the morning prayer on February 13, 2023, in the Lectio 365 daily devotional app created by 24-7 Prayer. Find out more and download the free app at www.24-7prayer.com/lectio-365.

way. The eureka moments and the exhilaration of noticing the ways you were changing. Recall the lows. The doubts and frustration at not having the time you hoped to spend with your giant. Remember when it felt like you had stumbled onto the wrong path, had hit a dead end, or weren't going anywhere at all. When it didn't seem like God was with you and when it felt like you could reach out and touch Him.

Even if you had never heard of this practice before embarking on the journey, think of the ways your life with God has grown, the relationships that have been mended, and the steps you've taken forward in your purpose. Take a moment to thank God for this gift!

If this journey can teach us anything, it's that there is always more. Just as God brought you this new practice of walking with giants, He is waiting for the right moment to surprise you with your next gift on your everlasting journey with Him.

May the Lord help you stay close and alert, and may you keep saying "Yes!" to His invitations.

JOURNAL

- Here at the end of the journey, what is God saying to you?

- What are you grateful for from the journey?

MILE MARKER

The giant journey offers natural moments to pause at the side of the trail. Take time to do this at the end of each month.

FINAL STEPS ON THE TRAIL

The walk with your giant doesn't end when the year is done. You are now forever friends connected by strong cords of the heart and spirit. You may not be walking the trail with them anymore, but they will still be with you. When you make mistakes, you will hear their words of wisdom. When you struggle, you will be strengthened by their example. When you walk into new places in your calling, you will be reminded of their courage and perseverance. And when you cross your earthly finish line, they will be there with a big hug to welcome you home.

As you conclude your journey, see the next section, "Finisterre—End of Journey Reflection," for a meaningful way to complete this special journey with your giant.

FINISTERRE—END OF
JOURNEY REFLECTION

Since we are surrounded by such a great cloud of witnesses, let us throw off everything that hinders and the sin that so easily entangles. And let us run with perseverance the race marked out for us, fixing our eyes on Jesus, the pioneer and perfecter of faith. For the joy set before him he endured the cross, scorning its shame, and sat down at the right hand of the throne of God.

—Hebrews 12:1–2

At the beginning of my journey with Fred, as I dreamed about how I wanted to finish, I thought of the Camino pilgrims reaching Santiago. When all the festivities are done, most make their way to the train depot and head to Madrid or Barcelona to fly home. But the wise ones don't end their pilgrimage so abruptly. Traveling a little farther west to the peaceful coastal town of Finisterre, they allow themselves a few days by the sea to rest, reflect, and give thanks, gleaning all they can from their sacred journey before regular life sweeps back in.

Now, as you complete your sacred journey, the same decision is before you: Will you abruptly toss aside the books, put away your journal, and resume regular life? Or will you head to a Finisterre of your own?

To show gratitude for the sacred gifts you have received on this journey, spend time in God's presence and give Him space to reveal anything else He would like to show you or what your journey should look like from here.

FINAL REFLECTION

Set aside an hour or perhaps even a day or two to wrap up your journey. Gather your book and any other materials about your giant and find your quiet place. Use the questions below as you are led. You can answer one, a few, all, or none. Just as your giant journey is unique, your final reflection will be as well. There's no right or wrong way to do it. Simply follow the leading of the Spirit.

Final Reflection Location:

Date of Final Reflection:

1. How is the Lord leading you to reflect on your journey? By using these prompts? Through free-flow journaling? Another way?

2. What were your hopes as you began this journey?

3. As you look back through your notes and think about your experiences this year, what books or other media most influenced your journey?

4. Which quotes from your giant have come back to you repeatedly?

5. Which spiritual practices inspired by your giant were especially meaningful to you?

6. What important people did your giant introduce you to?

7. What significant changes did you notice in your relationships?

8. What growth did you notice in your relationship with God?

9. Why do you think God led you to the giant He did?

10. How has the journey better equipped you to run your race?

11. How are you feeling led? Are you finished with your journey, or do you sense the Spirit nudging you to continue with your giant? Why or why not?

TRAVELOGUE

CLOSING THOUGHTS

Do you not know that in a race all the runners run [their very best to win], but only one receives the prize? Run [your race] in such a way that you may seize the prize and make it yours!

—1 Corinthians 9:24, AMP

We shouldn't emerge from this journey as carbon copies of our giants. Rather, the time spent with them should end with us drawing closer to God and becoming more of who He has created us to be. Even though this journey has centered on Fred, the goal of it is to lead us not into worshipping him but into worshipping more deeply the God who created him. Our answers should never be in our giants but in Christ in our giants.

For me, walking with Fred gave me confidence in the gifts God has called me to bring to the world. My journey enabled me to throw off the weights that hinder me and the sins tangling me up and to run the race set before me—just as Fred did—with my eyes more fixed on Jesus, the author and perfecter of our faith (Hebrews 12:1–2). I've realized that everything from my talents to my scars has been perfectly designed for the work I'm here to do.

Although I may not always feel impeccably equipped or exceedingly proficient, I can see from Fred's example that what I do in obedience— mixed with the Creator's plan—becomes a miracle. I've deepened my love for God and grown closer to family, friends, and neighbors by being attentive to those right in front of me and learning to love them just the way they are. I've developed a Christlike wonder as I've recovered my childlike self. I smile and laugh more often and appreciate the simple things more readily. I've let go of worry, knowing that I'm my

Abba Father's little girl and that I can reach up and put my hand into His. I've strengthened my experience of prayer and silence and established a greater connection to brothers and sisters in Christ.

My prayer is that your journey with Fred or whatever other giant you chose has been just as transformative and meaningful. I pray that this imperfect human has encouraged you to be more faithful and that God has used their example to strengthen you. As you continue your journey, may your love for God grow wider, higher, and deeper, and may your eyes be open to the gift of spiritual giants—a treasure trove that He has placed along our path.

Thinking of you, my fellow pilgrim.

"¡Ultreia et suseia!"
Onward and upward,
Lori

PILGRIM PRAYER

Oh Lord, my faithful guide, You have been with me every step of the journey. Thank You for the giants You have provided to equip and free us—and for making us more like Your Son. I praise You for all You have done and all You will do. Thank You for helping me grow closer to You through this journey. I'm so excited for the road ahead. My eyes are on You. I'm lacing up my boots to follow wherever You lead—all for Your kingdom and Your glory. Amen.

ACKNOWLEDGMENTS

They say it takes a village to raise a child. To create this book, it definitely took a neighborhood!

Like with most other things worth doing, I had no idea how much effort it would take to pull off this "I'm going to write a book!" thing when I first said it. As I come to the end now and look back at all who've been a part of it, I am overwhelmed. Fred's mother, Nancy, was known to encourage him whenever he was overwhelmed or afraid to "Look for the helpers. You will always find people who are helping."*

Those words ring true as I think about this book and all the helpers who've been there along the way. At every crossroads that seemed impossible, I would look around and see a helper waving me over with exactly what the book needed.

First, Sister Diane, Sister Carm, and the rest of the staff at the Dominican Center, who introduced me to this practice.

My Abba Sisters—Linda, my spiritual mentor, who first encouraged me to write and put wind in my sails along the way; and Julie, Sherri, and Donna, whose friendship and prayer carried me through.

The Breathe Writers Conference, which introduced me to the writing world and two very important Anns: Ann Byle and Ann Kroeker.

My writing communities at Hope*Writers and the Profitable Writer and our church blog team, who equipped me with everything I needed to enter the mysterious writing world, especially Kent Sanders and Ariel

---

* Aisha Harris, "The History of Mister Rogers' Powerful Message," Slate, April 16, 2013, https://slate.com/culture/2013/04/look-for-the-helpers-mister-rogers-quote-a-brief-history.html.

Curry for getting me through the daunting task of writing a book proposal. Yikes!

Cynthia Beach, who told me I had to come to Scriptoria when I hadn't even taken a college composition class, and my workshop group for their invaluable critique. Jon Sweeney and Cindy Bunch, who gave me my first opportunity to pitch and whose enthusiasm for this project convinced me that I had something valuable to share.

The three *Journey with a Giant* beta groups and our first leaders—Robert, Sherri, and Julie—for their invaluable feedback. And the amazing prayer team as well.

Leslie Calhoun and the incredible team at WaterBrook, who made the book into what it is and brought this powerful practice to the world. Your partnership has been a dream come true.

Ann Byle, who believed in the power of this idea from our first conversation, coached this newbie writer through each step, and then brought it to the marketplace as my agent.

My mom—my lifelong cheerleader—whose love, support, and prayers mean everything. My twin sister, Kelli, for her invaluable coaching and patience as I monopolized our phone conversations. My mother-in-law, who answered my regular SOS's and helped me keep my house clean and this big family going.

My kids, Drew, Kelsey, Eric, Geoff, Krystal, Jonathan, Victoria, Ross William, and Autumn, for their priceless cheers from the sidelines—"Go, Mom! You can do it!"—when I didn't know if I could.

My Bryan, who must be so tired of hearing about Fred, giants, Zoom meetings, and conferences and who has been my patron, coach, and counselor 24/7 for way longer than either one of us thought this would take. His belief in me and his support have been my greatest treasure. If there's an award for Best Neighbor, he definitely gets it!

And finally to God, the greatest Helper of all, behind the eyes of all the others, whose love and faithfulness make all our neighborhoods the wonderful places they are meant to be.

LORI G. MELTON is an author, spiritual director, and retreat leader with a lifelong passion for walking with God and fostering opportunities for others to grow in intimacy with Him. Though she was raised as an Episcopalian and attended Catholic school, she developed a personal faith in God through an Assemblies of God youth group and has spent her adult life in nondenominational Bible churches. As a result, one of her greatest strengths is her appreciation for diverse Christian denominations, which is reflected in the way her writing addresses believers of all Christian traditions.

After Lori had lived more than forty years as a devoted follower of Christ, God brought the spiritual giant practice into her life during a critical time of wrestling with her purpose. Instructed to choose a giant for one year of study during her spiritual direction training, she chose Evelyn Underhill, an English professor and retreat leader from the mid-twentieth century who taught the Church of England that everyone could hear the voice of God. In the following years of Lori's training, she chose a new giant—Francis of Assisi, the beloved Italian Catholic saint from the twelfth century—and experienced dramatic growth over her two years of walking alongside him.

With her training complete, Lori found herself continually drawn back to this practice. As others noticed the changes in her life, they began asking her to teach them how to walk with a giant. She wrote *Journey with a Giant* and began teaching spiritual giant workshops in response to those requests, presenting the practice through the engaging story of walking with her new giant, Mister Rogers.

Lori received her spiritual direction certification from the Dominican Center in Grand Rapids, Michigan, and is a member of Spiritual Directors International, the Association of Covenant Spiritual Directors, and Hope*Writers. Additionally, she and her husband, Bryan, are the founders and directors of the Sanctuary at Bear Creek Retreat Center in Allegan, Michigan, serving hundreds of people per year through their prayer cabin, other facilities, events, and website.

Still in awe that five sons and a daughter call her "Mom," Lori is the other half of a twin sister combination and loves nothing more than a hot mugga and a good laugh.

SPECIAL INVITATION

The only thing more fulfilling than walking with a giant yourself is sharing the journey with others. To receive your free downloadable *Journey with a Giant* discussion guide, go to lorigmelton.com/JWAGdiscuss.